ALSO BY ROBERT SPENCER

Holy Hell: Islam's Abuse of Women and the Infidels Who Enable It

Intifada on the Hudson: The Selling of Zohran Mamdani

Antisemitism: History and Myth

Muhammad: A Critical Biography

Empire of God: How the Byzantines Saved Civilization

The Sumter Gambit: How the Left Is Trying to Foment a Civil War

The Critical Qur'an: Explained from Key Islamic Commentaries and Contemporary Historical Research

Did Muhammad Exist?: An Inquiry into Islam's Obscure Origins—Revised and Expanded Edition

Obama and Trump: Who Was Better for America?

Rating America's Presidents: An America-First Look at Who Is Best, Who Is Overrated, and Who Was An Absolution Disaster

The Palestinian Delusion: The Catastrophic History of the Middle East Peace Process

The History of Jihad: From Muhammad to ISIS

Confessions of an Islamophobe

THE TRAGEDY OF ISLAM

FAILURE AND EXCUSES

ROBERT SPENCER

BOMBARDIER BOOKS

Published by Bombardier Books
An Imprint of Post Hill Press
ISBN: 979-8-88845-922-5
ISBN (eBook): 979-8-88845-923-2

The Tragedy of Islam:
Failure and Excuses

Cover Design by Jim Villaflores

This is a work of nonfiction. All people, locations, events, and situations are portrayed to the best of the author's memory.

BOMBARDIER BOOKS

Post Hill PRESS

Post Hill Press
New York • Nashville
posthillpress.com

Published in the United States of America
1 2 3 4 5 6 7 8 9 10

"Come to prayer! Come to success"—The Islamic call to prayer

Dedicated with love to all those who were
promised success and found only failure.

TABLE OF CONTENTS

CHAPTER ONE

IS ISLAM THE SOLUTION?

THE FAILURE OF ISLAM

For the entirety of the early part of the twenty-first century, Westerners have been consistently lectured about the superior morals and history of the culture that has given rise to numerous deadly terror attacks. This book exposes the contradictions of this demonstrably false narrative.

Some people, having been carefully instructed to believe that speech they don't like equals violence, or leads to it, will find the very idea of this book off-putting. How dare I, or anyone, even speculate as to whether or not Islam is a failure?

While books such as *Christianity Is Not Great: How Faith Fails* by the noted atheist polemicist John W. Loftus raise few eyebrows, criticizing Islam carries with it a particular stigma: it supposedly indicates that the one doing the criticizing hates Muslims, and wants to incite violence against them. Yet there is no reason why this should be so.

Societies consist of constellations of ideas. Whether these ideas are right or wrong, good or bad, those that become dominant in a society translate into actions. It is overly simplistic to say that allegedly offensive speech leads to violence, but there is nevertheless no doubt that ideas, beliefs and attitudes have definite effects, which can be observed and evaluated. In the case of Islam, that observation and lead to an inescapable conclusion: Islam is a failure.

Since our educational system has robbed a generation of Americans of the ability to make basic distinctions, it is necessary to note, at this point, that to say that Islam is a failure is not to say that every Muslim is a failure, or that Muslims in the aggregate are bad people. The distinction between Islam as a belief system and individual Muslims has been deliberately obscured in order to silence criticism of the belief system: to speak negatively of Islam, we have been told, is to endanger Muslims.

This is not only false, it also prevents us from doing the necessary work of evaluating ideas and beliefs—Islam as well as others—in order to determine whether we have really been wise to encourage their proliferation in American society. Many people will cheerfully avow that they want to see the influence of Christianity limited in various ways in American society, because they consider that influence baneful. No one charges them with "hate" or "incitement." We ought to have that discussion about Christianity. We ought to have one about Islam as well.

THE CURE TO WHAT AILS US

Everyone can see that the Western world is seriously ill. No one, however, agrees what should be done about it. Some say the solution need not be, and in fact is not, something new. According to many Muslims in the West today, the solution is actually something very old. Yet as old as it is, this solution has never been tried in most of the Western world: Islam.

Sheikh Raed Salah, leader of the Islamic Movement in Israel, preached on February 2, 2024, that America was on its way out, and that the world had to prepare accordingly: "The politicians who are asking about 'the day after' in Gaza have forgotten to ask themselves about 'the day after' in America—not only in Gaza. What about 'the day after' in America—after America has finished playing its role? America has grown old. It is old. It is on the verge of retirement. It is about to be admitted into a nursing home."[1]

The solution for America as well as for the rest of the world, said Salah, was the religion of Muhammad. He even claimed that Muhammad himself had prophesied an Islamic America: "The Prophet Muhammad has said: 'A small army of Muslims will conquer the white house, the house of Kisar [the Persian ruler].'"[2] In case any of his listeners missed his point, he continued, "Ever since the days of Adam and to day—this is 2024—we have never known of any house that was built and named 'the White House,' except for the 'White House' in Washington." He didn't bother to disclose to his audience why a Persian ruler was occupying America's Executive Mansion. Instead, Salah drove home the point that Islam was in America's future: "Perhaps this *hadith* is clear evidence that the future caliphate [that will follow] the ways of the prophets will lead to the spreading of Islam, and

1 "Israeli Islamist Leader Sheikh Raed Salah: The World Must Prepare For The 'Day After America,' Which Has Grown Old And Is About To Retire; Islam Will Enter The White House And Will Conquer Europe Through Da'wa," MEMRI, February 2, 2024, https://www.memri.org/reports/israeli-islamist-leader-sheikh-raed-salah-world-must-prepare-day-after-america-which-has. Accessed October 30, 2024.

2 Ibid.

Islam will enter every home in every continent without exception, including every home in America."[3]

In the waning months of the Biden administration, with both parties predicting the end of American "democracy" (spoiler: it's a republic) if the other side won the November presidential election, Salah was not remotely alone in predicting this. On May 3, 2024, a student at the University of Chicago, Mohammad Nusairat, preached a Friday sermon for the university's Muslim Students Association chapter. "America," he declared, "is the cancer. America, the American government, secularism, democracy, capitalism, these are cancers that have spread their illness all over the world—in America and in the Middle East."

Nusairat had an alternative ready: "Now Muslims are tired of this cancer. They're tired of the American government. They're tired of democracy. They want to see a new way of life. And as Muslims, we have to understand, that we have that new way of life."[4] Muhammad, Nusairat explained, "was sent as a mercy for all of mankind. He was sent as a mercy. Why? Because the way of life he brought, will bring that mercy. The way of life he brought, will bring that tranquility, to Muslims and non-Muslims. Non-Muslims won't have to worry about the issues they worry about now. You won't have to. Because Islam is a just religion that has come to be implemented upon society."[5]

These were not new ideas any more than Islam was a new solution. Nusairat's words echoed the assessment of one of the

---

3 Ibid.

4 "University Of Illinois Chicago Students At Friday Sermon: America, Democracy, Secularism Are A Cancer; Muslims Have A New, Just Way Of Life That Will Bring Tranquility To Muslims And Non-Muslims; The People Capable Of Freeing Al-Aqsa Are In This Room; May Allah Make Us Among The Liberators Of The Al-Aqsa Mosque," MEMRI, May 3, 2024, https://www.memri.org/tv/university-illinois-chicago-friday-sermon-america-democracy-cancer-islam-new-way-life. Accessed October 30, 2024.

5 Ibid.

most profound and consequential Muslim thinkers of the twentieth century, the Egyptian Muslim Brotherhood theorist Sayyid Qutb. In his influential 1964 book *Milestones*, Qutb offers Islam as the way out of the blind alleys of capitalism and Communism: "Mankind today is on the brink of a precipice," Qutb wrote, "not because of the danger of complete annihilation which is hanging over its head—this being just a symptom and not the real disease—but because humanity is devoid of those vital values which are necessary not only for its healthy development but also for its real progress."[6]

The West, in Qutb's view, offered no viable cure to this disease, and was aware of its own failure: "Even the Western world realizes that Western civilization is unable to present any healthy values for the guidance of mankind. It knows that it does not possess anything which will satisfy its own conscience and justify its existence."[7]

At the height of the Cold War, Qutb thought that both of the two great ideas that dominated the world and were vying for hegemony over it—Communism and capitalism—were spiritually vacuous and intellectually bankrupt: "Democracy in the West has become infertile to such an extent that it is borrowing from the systems of the Eastern bloc, especially in the economic system, under the name of socialism. It is the same with the Eastern bloc. Its social theories, foremost among which is Marxism, in the beginning attracted not only a large number of people from the East but also from the West, as it was a way of life based on a creed."[8]

6 Sayyid Qutb, Milestones (Cedar Rapids, Iowa: The Mother Mosque Foundation, n.d.), 7.
7 Ibid.
8 Ibid.

It may seem strange at first glance to offer a religion as the solution to the failure or inadequacy of two socioeconomic systems. It must be remembered that Islam is much more than just a religion in the Western sense. It is a total way of life, offering a political system, a social system, and even an economic system. Islamic apologists brag about this in making negative comparisons of Islam with Christianity; the latter, they say, offers only a handful of vague moral principles, while Islam encompasses literally every detail of human behavior. There is no aspect of human activity that Islamic law doesn't cover. As such, Islam is indeed a worthy competitor and alternative to Communism and Christianity, for it doesn't just orient human beings to the deity, but to one another as well, regulating every aspect of human interaction.

At a time when many Western intellectuals were embracing Marxism, Qutb asserted that "now Marxism is defeated on the plane of thought, and if it is stated that not a single nation in the world is truly Marxist, it will not be an exaggeration."[9] Marxism was, in fact, a failure, because "on the whole this theory conflicts with man's nature and its needs. This ideology prospers only in a degenerate society or in a society which has become cowed as a result of some form of prolonged dictatorship."[10] In Qutb's view, "the failure of the system of collective farming" was just one aspect of "the failure of a system which is against human nature."[11]

Having already demonstrated, at least to his own satisfaction, that capitalism was not the answer, Qutb declared, "It is essential for mankind to have new leadership!"[12] The source of

---

[9] Ibid.
[10] Ibid.
[11] Ibid.
[12] Ibid.

this new direction would be Islam: "If we look at the sources and foundations of modern ways of living, it becomes clear that the whole world is steeped in *Jahiliyyah* [Ignorance of the Divine guidance], and all the marvelous material comforts and high-level inventions do not diminish this ignorance. This *Jahiliyyah* is based on rebellion against God's sovereignty on earth. It transfers to man one of the greatest attributes of God, namely sovereignty, and makes some men lords over others."[13] Islam, however, did away with all that, and preached the radical equality of all people as slaves of Allah. This vision, Qutb thought, would do away with racism, class warfare, and a host of other ills of both capitalist and Communist societies.

THE GLOBAL ISLAMIC REVOLUTION

A twentieth-century Pakistani Muslim intellectual, Sayyid Abul A'la Maududi, shared Qutb's contention that Islam offered a solution to the blind alleys and dead ends of contemporary thought. Founder of the Jamaat-e-Islami (Islamic Party), which was dedicated to imposing full observance of Islamic law, Maududi remains one of the most influential Islamic thinkers of the modern age. His writings on the Qur'an and political Islam are read and revered worldwide to this day.

Central to Maududi's vision of the world was the fact that Islam was not just a religion, but a political system, and one that in his view should be unapologetic about being supremacist and violent:

> In common terminology, "religion" means nothing more than a hotch potch of some beliefs,

[13] Ibid., 10–11.

> prayers and rituals. If this is what "religion" means, then, it should, indeed, be a private affair. You should be free to entertain any belief and worship any deity whom your conscience is ready to accept. If you are over-zealous and ardent devotees of this type of religion, go and preach it to the whole world and engage yourselves in declamations with the protagonists of other religions. There is no reason why you should take up a sword. Do you wish to convert people to your faith by killing them? We are forced to admit the point that if you regard Islam as a religion in the conventional meaning of the term and if, indeed, Islam be a conventional type of religion, the necessity for "Jihad" cannot be justified.[14]

Writing at a time when Western intellectuals were first becoming enamored of Communism, Maududi appropriated the language of Marxism for his own political program: "The truth is that Islam is not the name of a 'Religion,' nor is 'Muslim' the title of a 'Nation.' In reality Islam is a revolutionary ideology and programme which seeks to alter the social order of the whole world and rebuild it in conformity with its own tenets and ideals. 'Muslim' is the title of that International Revolutionary Party organized by Islam to carry into effect its revolutionary programme. And 'Jihad' refers to that revolutionary struggle and

---

14 Abul A'la Maududi, Jihad In Islam, (Beirut: The Holy Koran Publishing House, 1939), 3–4.

utmost exertion which the Islamic Party brings into play to achieve this objective."[15]

Maududi's program was internationalist: "Islam has no vested interest in promoting the cause of this or that Nation. The hegemony of this or that State on the face of this earth is irrelevant to Islam."[16] Nationalism was anathema to this global vision: "Islam wishes to destroy all States and Governments anywhere on the face of the earth which are opposed to the ideology and programme of Islam regardless of the country or the Nation which rules it."[17]

Once all states and governments that didn't operate according to Islamic principles were destroyed, Islam would replace them: "The purpose of Islam is to set up a State on the basis of its own ideology and programme, regardless of which Nation assumes the role of the standard-bearer of Islam or the rule of which nation is undermined in the process of the establishment of an ideological Islamic State."[18]

Although Maududi apparently envisions the destruction of existing states by force, ultimately this conflict will be for the good of mankind in general: "Islam requires the earth—not just a portion, but the whole planet—not because the sovereignty over the earth should be wrested from one Nation or several Nations and vested in one particular Nation, but because the entire mankind should benefit from the ideology and welfare programme or what would be truer to say from 'Islam' which is the programme of well-being for all humanity."[19] Jihad was the mechanism by which the earth would be given this tremendous gift: "Towards

[15] Ibid., 5.
[16] Ibid., 6.
[17] Ibid.
[18] Ibid.
[19] Ibid., 7.

this end, Islam wishes to press into service all forces which can bring about a revolution and a composite term for the use of all these forces is 'Jihad.'"[20]

The Islamic vision was, in Maududi's view, deeply and quintessentially humanitarian, even when it involved Muslims waging violent jihad in order to destroy the existing order: "The 'Jihad' of Islam is not merely a 'struggle'; it is a 'struggle for the Cause of God'. 'For the Cause of God is an essential condition for 'Jihad' in Islam.... All such work as is undertaken for the collective well-being of mankind and in which the functionary has no vested interest in the present world, his sole interest being to win the favour of God, is regarded in Islam as an 'act in the way of God.'"[21]

Everyone would come under the purview of the new global order: "The call of Islam is not addressed to the workers, and holders, peasants or industrialists; it is directed to the whole of human race."[22] It would require those who held power to be forced to relinquish it, for they had no right to it in Maududi's frankly theocratic vision: "No one," he says, "has the right to become a self-appointed ruler of men and issue orders and prohibitions on his own volition and authority. To acknowledge the personal authority of a human being as the source of commands and prohibitions is tantamount to admitting him as the sharer in the Powers and Authority of God. And this is the root of all evils in the universe."[23]

The destruction of the existing governing powers of the earth would be tantamount to nothing less than "evil and contumacy"

---

20 Ibid.
21 Ibid., 7–8.
22 Ibid., 11.
23 Ibid., 11–12.

being actually "wiped out" from the earth, and the law of Allah being "enforced in the world."[24] As a matter of fidelity to Allah, the Muslim Party is accordingly "left with no other choice except to capture State Authority, for an evil system takes root and flourishes under the patronage of an evil government and a pious cultural order can never be established until the authority of Government is wrested from the wicked and transferred into the hands of the reformers."[25]

The mission is not complete if all the earth is not united in the new order: "the Muslim Party for reasons of both general welfare of humanity and self-defense…should not rest content with establishing the Islamic System of Government in one territory alone, but to extend the sway of [the] Islamic System all around as far as its resources can carry it."[26]

Once the Muslims attain political power, they will begin the great work of creating a just society, which will necessarily involve the ending some practices that were previously tolerated or even celebrated: "For instance, as soon as the Ummah of Islam captures state power it will ban all forms of business prosecuted on the basis of usury or interest; it will not permit the practice of gambling; it will curb all forms of business and financial dealings which are forbidden by Islamic law; it will close down all dens of prostitution and other vices and for all; it will make it obligatory for non-Muslim women to observe the minimum standards of modesty in dress as required by Islamic law and will forbid them to go about displaying their beauty like the days of ignorance; the Muslim Party will clamp censorship on the Cinema. The Islamic government with a view to securing general welfare of

[24] Ibid., 10.
[25] Ibid., 19.
[26] Ibid., 23.

the public and for reasons of self-defence will not permit such cultural activities as may be permissible in non-Muslim creeds, but which, from the viewpoint of Islam are corrosive of moral fibres and fatal."[27]

Eighty-five years after Maududi articulated this vision, an imam in Tuskegee, Alabama was likewise certain that Islam held out for mankind the way out of the misery of *Jahiliyyah*, and equally certain that it would indeed take over. At a Juneteenth commemoration on June 22, 2024, he announced, "We are going to have to prepare ourselves to run the world."[28] The imam, unnamed in a video that the area Muslims published on Facebook, added, "The real hope for America is for Muslims in America to come together and to work not only with other Muslims but with people who are concerned about the lives of our people.... Don't take it lightly. I don't believe America can be saved unless we save it.... It is on us to remake America. Do you understand? It's on us, and that means we have to create a collective mind, a collective effort.... We have work to do, y'all."[29]

But can Islam really save America? Does it really offer a solution to the grave illnesses of Western society?

MATERIAL PROSPERITY

To answer that question, we must first consider what it means for America to be "saved." If a majority of Americans accepted Islam, men such as Salah, Nusairat, and the Alabama imam, as well as

---

27 Ibid., 27–8.

28 "Juneteenth Commemoration At Tuskegee, Alabama Mosque: Muslims Must Remake America, It Cannot Be Saved Unless We Save It; We Must Prepare Ourselves To Run The World," MEMRI, June 22, 2024, https://www.memri.org/tv/tuskegee-alabama-muslims-prepare-to-run-the-world-real-hope-muslims-remake-america. Accessed October 30, 2024.

29 Ibid.

Qutb, might think that Allah would turn his wrath away from the nation, and the Americans who converted would be spared the fires of hell. Contrary to this widespread assumption among politicians and media trendsetters, however, that religions are all essentially interchangeable and equivalent in whatever effects they may have on society, an Islamic America would be radically different from what it is today.

In keeping with Islamic law, a majority-Muslim United States would likely criminalize behaviors that Islam forbids: the sale and consumption of alcohol and pork, the use of interest in financial transactions, and more. The veil would almost certainly be made mandatory for women, as it is in the Islamic Republic of Iran and other Sharia states. Certain behaviors, such as homosexual acts, fornication, and adultery could also be criminalized, while polygamy would be legalized. All this would, of course, have reverberations throughout the society that would affect virtually every area.

In consequence, a turn to Islam would change America utterly. But would it improve it? In the eyes of these Muslim thinkers, the answer would be a decisive yes, bringing not just spiritual health, but other elements of societal well-being, including even economic health and material prosperity. This promise is embedded in the Qur'an itself, which tells Muslims, "O you who believe, endure, outdo all others in endurance, be ready, and observe your duty to Allah, so that you may succeed." (3:200) The righteous will not just succeed by gaining a place in paradise. The Qur'an's promise applies to this world as well as the next. Regarding the blessed, "Allah gave them the reward of this world and the good reward of the hereafter. Allah loves those who do good deeds." (3:148).

Those who turn away from the divine commands will likewise suffer, as this threat applies to this world as well as the next: "And whoever becomes a renegade and dies in his disbelief, they are the ones whose works have failed both in this world and the hereafter. They are the rightful companions of the fire, they will remain in it." (2:217) Sayyid Qutb accordingly concludes: "As long as a believer continues to trust in God's grace, he shall never be disappointed."[30]

These promises mean that the assertions about Islam being the solution to America's problems can actually be tested. There are numerous states throughout history and today that have imposed Sharia tenets and enforced them stringently. If Islam is the solution, we should expect to see Sharia states among the economic powerhouses of the world, as the true believers in Allah reap the blessings of obedience to his commands. This should hold true both historically and today.

Yet it is not the case. Among Sharia states, Saudi Arabia has the highest Gross National Income (GNI), and even that country, with its fantastically rich oil sheikhs, is not in the top ten in the world in GNI. Its prosperity, moreover, clearly stems more from striking oil than from something intrinsic to Islam, for if it were due to Islam, other Sharia states would approach it in wealth.

Now, as is often the case with scriptural promises of all sorts, these Qur'anic promises of earthly prosperity may end up giving way to delays or reinterpretations of various kinds. The relative poverty of Sharia states doesn't prove that Islam is false and Allah an illusion any more than the wealth of Sharia states in the past showed that the religion was true. Still, if Islam is the solution

30 Sayyid Qutb, In the Shade of the Qur'an (Fi Zilal al-Qur'an), Volume 1, M. A. Salahi and A. A. Shamis, trans. (Leicester, United Kingdom: The Islamic Foundation, 1999), 261.

to the ills of the West and of the world at large, we should see it working in the societies where it is most faithfully implemented, for there is a correlation between the core beliefs of a population and its productivity, and hence its prosperity. All of this can be subject to a variety of factors, but that doesn't change the basic fact that what one believes affects how one behaves, and writ large across an entire society, the dominant belief system can make a massive difference in what the members of any given society spend their time doing.

NO WORK ETHIC

The connection between the widely held beliefs and assumptions of a society and its material condition has been recognized for well over a century. It was in 1904 that the German social scientist Max Weber noted that "a glance at the occupational statistics of any country of mixed religious composition brings to light with remarkable frequency a situation which has several times provoked discussion in the Catholic press and literature, and in Catholic congresses in Germany, namely, the fact that business leaders and owners of capital, as well as the higher grades of skilled labor, and even more the higher technically and commercially trained personnel of modern enterprises, are overwhelmingly Protestant."[31]

Weber saw this as no mere accident or coincidence. He quotes Benjamin Franklin at length, enjoining hard work and frugality: "Remember, that *time is money*. He that can earn ten shillings a day by his labor, and goes abroad, or sits idle, one half of that day, though he spends but sixpence during his diversion or idleness,

[31] Max Weber, The Protestant Ethic and the Spirit of Capitalism, Talcott Parsons, trans. (London and New York: Routledge, 1992), 3.

ought not to reckon that the only expense; he has really spent, or rather thrown away, five shillings besides."[32] Weber saw the root of these ideas in the religion in which Franklin was raised:

> If we thus ask, why should "money be made out of men," Benjamin Franklin himself, although he was a colorless deist, answers in his autobiography with a quotation from the Bible, which his strict Calvinistic father drummed into him again and again in his youth: "Seest thou a man diligent in his business? He shall stand before kings" (Prov. xxii. 29). The earning of money within the modern economic order is, so long as it is done legally, the result and the expression of virtue and proficiency in a calling; and this virtue and proficiency are, as it is now not difficult to see, the real Alpha and Omega of Franklin's ethic, as expressed in the passages we have quoted, as well as in all his works without exception.[33]

Weber's primary contention was that the Protestant world view sanctified human labor, leading to the relative prosperity of predominantly Protestant states. Whatever may be the merits, or lack thereof, of Weber's argument, his insight into how widely held beliefs could have an impact on societies as a whole, and particularly upon their ability or inability to prosper, is important and undeniable.

---

32 Ibid., 14.
33 Ibid., 18–19.

How, then, do Islamic beliefs affect the societies in which they constitute the dominant ideology? One clear difference between Islam and the Northern European Protestantism of Max Weber's day is that Islam does not inculcate a work ethic. According to Islamic tradition, Muhammad, the prophet of Islam, proclaimed himself a prophet in the Arabian city of Mecca in the year 610, and over the next twelve years in Mecca, amassed a small group of followers. It was not until after the *hijrah* (migration) to Medina in the year 622, however, that Muhammad began to oversee the construction of the first Islamic society. Indeed, to this day, the Islamic calendar numbers as the Year One the date not of Muhammad's birth or death, or the year in which tradition states that he proclaimed himself a prophet. Rather, the first year of Islam is the first year in Medina, when the Islamic society was first established.

Yet Muhammad did not enjoin his followers to begin to cultivate the land, or to become merchants or tradesmen. Instead, he directed them to raid the caravans of the Quraysh, the polytheistic Arabs of Mecca who, though they were Muhammad's friends and relatives, had rejected his claim to be a prophet. He exiled the Jewish tribes of Medina and then attacked them at the oasis of Khaybar, where they had taken refuge, and ordered the torture of the leader of the community until he revealed where the treasury was hidden. Once the warring tribes of Arabia were subdued, Muhammad turned against the Roman Empire's outposts in northern Arabia.

The Roman Empire was Christian. Muhammad accordingly received a revelation commanding the Muslims to fight even against the "people of the book" (that is, Jews, Christians, and a few other groups): "Fight against those who do not believe in Allah or the last day, and do not forbid what Allah and his messenger have forbidden, and do not follow the religion of truth, even if they are among the people of the book, until they pay the *jizya* [a head tax] with willing submission and feel themselves subdued." (Qur'an 9:29) Muhammad's second successor as spiritual, political and military leader of the Muslim community, Umar ibn al-Khattab, told the Muslims to be sure to collect the jizya, for the Muslims depended upon it: "I advise you to fulfill Allah's Convention (made with the Dhimmis) as it is the convention of your Prophet and the source of the livelihood of your dependents (i.e. the taxes from the Dhimmis.)"[34]

This advice has been heeded throughout Islamic history, to the extent that it became a cultural habit.

[34] Muhammad ibn Ismail al-Bukhari, Sahih al-Bukhari, vol. 4, bk. 58, no. 3162, https://sunnah.com/bukhari:3162. Accessed October 30, 2024.

CHAPTER TWO

THE ISLAMIC ETHIC AND THE SPIRIT OF PARASITISM

WORK IS A CURSE

The caliph Umar's admonition to the Muslims to always be sure to collect the jizya was no offhand remark, but a guiding principle. The subjugation of the people of the book has indeed been the primary source of income for Islamic polities throughout history, and their fortunes have risen and fallen with the wealth or poverty of the subjugated communities. The best life has never been envisioned as one in which one labors hard and well and then enjoys the fruits of one's labor. Instead, the ideal has always been to enjoy the fruits of the labor of others.

In his groundbreaking study *The Arab Mind*, the twentieth-century historian and anthropologist Raphael Patai notes that "Aversion to manual labor, in particular work that involves dirtying one's hands, is another Bedouin attitude that has widely influenced the Arab mind. Among the nomads to this day there is a notion that engaging in agriculture or any craft is dishonoring. This preference for a life of leisure, or, if that is impractical, as it is for the overwhelming majority of Arabs, then at least for work that does not involve the use of muscle power bears importantly on both the historical development of the Arab culture and the processes of its Westernization."[35]

This is not just a trait of the Bedouin or the Arab, but is quite common among Muslims in general. Patai explains further, "This attitude can be expressed very succinctly: Work is a curse. It represents the diametrical opposite of the Protestant ethic, which considers work as a good, as something that ennobles man. In the Middle Eastern ethic, from pre-biblical times down to the present, the ideal has always been to escape the curse of work, to earn, or rather to acquire, riches through a stroke of luck, by finding a treasure, by finding favor in the eyes of a king, by buying something cheap and selling it at a high price, by being helped by a jinni."[36]

Or by a dhimmi. This can be seen clearly in the rise and decline of one of the most successful Islamic states in history, the Ottoman Empire.

THE OTTOMANS: A CASE STUDY

Nearly a millennium after Umar reminded the Muslims always to be sure to collect the jizya (*cizye* in Turkish), the collection of this tax was critical for the functioning of the Ottoman Empire, which considered its sultans, as the caliphs of Muslim *umma*, to be successors of Muhammad as much as Umar was. The *cizye* was

35 Raphael Patai, The Arab Mind, revised edition (Long Island City, New York: Haverleigh Press, 2002), 120.

36 Ibid., 122.

essential to the workings of the Ottoman Empire. Contemporary historian Tom Papademetriou notes that "the collection of the *cizye* was of such great importance that an accounting bureau for the poll tax (*cizye muhasebesi kalemi*) was created around 1569–70 and was run by dozens of scribes who filed the *cizye* registers from throughout the empire."[37] In fact, "the *cizye*, because it was a flat fee tax paid per non-Muslim household, became the largest revenue source in the sixteenth century."[38]

This was the period during which the empire was at its political height: steadily expanding into Eastern Europe while threatening Central and Western Europe as well, and at the same time becoming a formidable naval power. The sultan Suleiman the Magnificent conquered Belgrade in 1521 and Rhodes the following year. In 1529, he besieged Vienna, but had to withdraw, not because Ottoman forces had been bested on the battlefield, but because his supply lines were stretched to the breaking point. He did, however, take Algiers that year, and Tripoli in 1551.

Through all this, the Ottoman Empire's largest revenue source was the tax that it levied upon non-Muslims, in accord with the Qur'anic dictate. The Jewish and Christian communities financed the confident Ottoman expansion into Europe and North Africa, making the name of the empire strike fear in the inhabitants of all the surrounding regions.

The Ottomans faced the task of governing their massive empire with considerably less enthusiasm than they brought to the task of conquering the lands that constituted it. "The Turks," states contemporary historian Lucien Gubbay, were "comparatively

---

37 Tom Papademetriou, Render Unto the Sultan: Power, Authority, and the Greek Orthodox Church in the Early Ottoman Centuries (Oxford: Oxford University Press, 2015), 141.

38 Ibid.

few in number" in comparison to the vast numbers of captive peoples within the empire.[39] Thus they were "faced with the formidable task of stabilizing and then governing the vast empire conquered by the brilliance of their armies. In many places they took over towns and a countryside partly emptied by the ravages of war. In the Balkans, the Mediterranean islands and Anatolia they also took over a resentful and potentially untrustworthy Christian population."[40]

Just as Umar had directed so long before, the Ottomans saw the conquered people primarily as a source of revenue. "The Turks were not colonists and made no attempt to cultivate the conquered lands and put down roots: their Empire existed primarily as a source of wealth for the Sultan and the ruling class surrounding him."[41] The Ottomans had no more interest in becoming farmers or merchants than Muhammad did when he moved to Medina: "As a nation of Islamic warriors, it was beneath Turkish dignity to engage in occupations other than the army, the government and the mosque. They actively despised commerce, manufacture and the crafts. Furthermore, as strict Muslims they avoided contact with unbelievers, which effectively debarred them from diplomacy, money-changing, banking and international trade."[42] They thus depended upon the money they collected from the Jews and Christians, as they themselves engaged in few activities that generated any income other than conquest and plunder.

39 Lucien Gubbay, "The Rise, Decline and Attempted Regeneration of the Jews of the Ottoman Empire," European Judaism: A Journal for the New Europe, Spring 2000, Vol. 33, No. 1, The Exile of Jerusalem Which Is In Sepharad (Oxford: Berghahn Books, 2000), 60.

40 Ibid.

41 Ibid., 61.

42 Ibid.

The Ottomans enlisted the Jews of the empire to do the jobs that they considered to be beneath them, because the Christians—bitter over the Ottoman conquest and destruction of the Roman (Byzantine) Empire—were considered far less trustworthy. The Ottomans "welcomed the services of Jews, adept in the occupations they disdained, and much preferred them to Christians—for Jews, totally loyal to the Ottoman state, had no love for the Sultan's Christian enemies in Europe and the Byzantine Empire."[43]

Yet both were always subject to the institutionalized discrimination of the *dhimma*, the subordinate status that Islamic law mandated for Jews and Christians. Besides having to pay the jizya, or *cizye*, they had to wear clothing that clearly distinguished them from Muslims, and couldn't build new churches or synagogues without the permission of the sultan. The dhimmis were also forbidden to hold authority over Muslims,—thus relegated to the most menial tasks in society (although that law was frequently ignored).

Because the Jews were performing a valuable service for the empire and the Christians were viewed with suspicion, these rules were often relaxed for the Jews—except for the payment of the *cizye*, which was always scrupulously collected.[44] Nevertheless, Papademetriou notes that "by the seventeenth century," the *cizye* was no longer the empire's principal revenue source: "additional taxes, the extraordinary levies (*avariz*), became more important to the overall income."[45]

43 Ibid.
44 Ibid., 62.
45 Papademetriou, op. cit.

DECLINE

Why did the *cizye* decline in importance? The answer is simple: one cannot get blood from a stone. The laws of the *dhimma* required that Islam's supremacy be constantly maintained. While individual Jews and even some Christians were able to attain great positions of power and influence and amass great wealth, for the most part their communities were gradually and steadily impoverished as they continued to pay the *cizye* year after year, while facing, as subject people, reduced earning possibilities.

The Ottoman Empire was thus caught in a downward spiral that had a precise and specific cause: Islam. Its teachings about how Allah blessed and rewarded warfare and conquest to expand the domains that were ruled by his divine law had provided the impetus for the empire's growth and expansion. Once it was established, however, Islam offered no worldview that could sustain it other than further growth, for the empire depended upon the taxes that the subject people paid into the treasury.

Islam also mandated that those subject peoples be constantly reminded of their subjugation. One primary way this was done was to stipulate that no member of a subject group could hold authority over a Muslim, thus closing off some lucrative careers. This rule was often ignored, and also many subject peoples were able to employ others of their own religion.

Over time, however, its effects were inevitably felt. As generation after generation went by, the Jews and Christians of the Ottoman Empire became progressively more impoverished, and as they did, this chief source of revenue began to dry up, and the more the empire had to depend upon other sources of income, including taxes on Muslims. However, these could never be as high as taxes on the subject peoples, or the *cizye* would no longer serve as a reminder of subjugation.

This was when the empire began to decline. The high-water mark of the empire's expansion into Eastern Europe was when the Ottomans tried and failed to take Vienna in 1683. In 1686 it lost Buda, and in 1699 it ceded what it controlled of Hungary to the Austrian Empire. By the early 1800s, the death throes of the empire had begun. Serbia and Greece revolted. The French took Algeria. In order to gain the support of the British and French against the Russians in the Crimean War in 1853, the Ottomans agreed to abolish the *cizye* altogether and emancipate the subject people (although many Jews and Christians within the empire felt scant improvement from this).

The Ottoman Empire allied with the Germans and Austrians during World War I, finally collapsing a few years after that war ended. The economic exhaustion of the Jewish and Christian communities was by no means the sole cause of the Ottomans' decline. Gubbay notes that "Turkey began to decay from within after the death of Suleiman the Magnificent in 1566. The sultans who succeeded him lacked the ability of his ten brilliant predecessors. Spoilt by the wealth that flowed so effortlessly into their coffers, they grew increasingly decadent and devoted far more time to court intrigue and the affairs of the harem than to government."[46] Corruption became widespread, leading to a decline in the effectiveness of Ottoman control from Constantinople, which in turn led to a weakening of the bonds that tied the provinces to the sultan and the empire. Crime and contempt for authority increased. Once the decline began, no one seemed to have the means or will to reverse it.

46 Gubbay, op. cit., 63.

If the Ottomans had not considered commerce, manufacture, and the crafts as beneath them, they might have been able to arrest and even reverse this decline. They might have been able to develop reliable sources of income that didn't depend upon impoverishing either the *dhimmis* or their own people, or forever attempting to conquer new lands to shore up the tax base by reducing new populations to *dhimmi* status.

It was Islam, however, that precluded that possibility. The Ottomans were entangled in a contradiction: they depended upon the *dhimmis* for their income, but they meanwhile had to keep the *dhimmis* in a second-class status that reduced their ability to earn money.

THE ABOLITION OF THE *DHIMMA* AND THE DEATH OF THE EMPIRE

After its long period of decline, the empire's death was hastened by the abolition of *dhimmi* status altogether. The Ottomans did not do this willingly. In 1842, the British ambassador to Constantinople, Stratford Canning, lodged a protest with the sultan Abdulmecid over the execution of two men who had run afoul of Islam's death penalty for apostasy by converting to Christianity. Canning asked the caliph to "give his royal word that henceforward neither should Christianity be insulted in his dominions, nor should Christians be in any way persecuted for their religion."[47] Since Abdulmecid sought Britain's help against the Russians, who were encroaching on Ottoman domains, he was open to Canning's appeal. While the British and French allied with the Ottomans

47 Lord Kinross, The Ottoman Centuries: The Rise and Fall of the Turkish Empire (New York: Morrow Quill Publishers, 1977), 477.

against Russia during the Crimean War, they kept up the pressure on Constantinople to ease its restrictions upon the *dhimmis*. The Ottomans ultimately relented; in the Hatt-i Humayun decree of 1856, Abdulmecid enacted the Tanzimat reforms, declaring a radical new idea: the equality before the law of all imperial subjects, including even Jews and Christians. The *cizye* was abolished.

These reforms turned out to be more a matter of appearance than reality. The British consul James H. Skene wrote in 1859 that "the Christian subjects of the sultan at Aleppo still live in a state of terror."[48] James Brant, another consul from London, in July 1860 lamented "the inability of the Sultans [sic] Government to protect its Christian subjects" from the rage of Muslim mobs.[49] A third British consul, James Finn, wrote that "oppression against Christians usually begins with the fanatic populace, but it is neither repressed nor punished by the Government."[50]

Yet while the former dhimmi communities still suffered from discrimination and occasional violence, the *cizye* was no longer collected. In the 1860s, the grand vizier Ali Pasha offered Sultan Abdulaziz some advice about how to revitalize the imperial economy: the Muslims must go to work. "Muslims must," Ali Pasha declared, "like the Christians, devote themselves to [commercial] agriculture, trade, industry and crafts. Labor is the only durable capital. Let us put ourselves to work, Sire, that is the only way to safety for us. There is still time to liberate the Muslim population from obligations which benefit the Christians."[51]

48 Bat Ye'or, The Decline of Eastern Christianity Under Islam: From Jihad to Dhimmitude (Madison, New Jersey: Fairleigh Dickinson University Press, 1996), 399–400.

49 Ibid., 406.

50 Ibid., 417.

51 Caroline Finkel, Osman's Dream: The History of the Ottoman Empire (New York: Basic Books, 2007), 470–1.

It was too late. Islam dictated that the *dhimmis* did the work, while the Muslims enjoyed its fruits. To instill a work ethic in the Ottoman Muslims would have been a labor of decades, beginning with early childhood education. Instead, the empire entered its death throes. Islam had created the Ottoman Empire; Islam also killed it.

This doesn't mean that no one works in Muslim countries, but work is not generally valued as something that is good in itself and can bring blessings upon the worker. The ideal situation is one in which the Muslims do not work, and the non-Muslims serve them. Once the non-Muslims can no longer sustain the Muslims at the level to which they have become accustomed, the Muslims have no reliable way to maintain themselves at the same level of prosperity. Their societies go into decline at that point.

Mustafa Kemal Ataturk, the founder of secular Turkey, saw this clearly, and modeled his post-Ottoman state on the democracies of Western Europe that had emerged victorious in World War I. "Islam," he said, "this theology of an immoral Arab, is a dead thing."[52] Seeing nothing around him but the ruin that Islam had created, he was determined that his new Turkish state would be built on a stronger, more sustainable foundation, one that would not destroy itself in its own contradictions.

(Ataturk was wrong; Islam was by no means dead. Turkey was still filled with people who believed that no state was legitimate unless it scrupulously implemented Islamic law; three quarters of a century after Ataturk destroyed the last Islamic caliphate, these people would find a sturdy champion in Recep Tayyip Erdogan, who set Turkey on a path toward discarding Kemalist secularism and recovering Ottoman glory.)

52 H. C. Armstrong, The Gray Wolf (London: Penguin Books, 1937), 205.

CHAPTER THREE

FAILED SOCIETIES

ISLAMIC INDIA: ANOTHER FAILED SOCIETY

The decline and fall of the Mughal empire in India follows the same pattern. In 711, the Arab general Muhammad ibn Qasim invaded Sindh (modern-day western Pakistan). This began the jihad conquest of India. However, India could not be conquered in the same way as the Christian lands of North Africa and the Middle East had been. The Qur'an stipulated that the jizya should be collected from the "people of the book": primarily Jews, Christians, and Zoroastrians. The appellation meant that these groups had received a legitimate revelation from Allah, although Muslims contended that they had dared to corrupt those revelations. Despite this supreme act of rebellion, they still received preferential status over other groups the Muslims conquered: they could continue to practice their ancestral religions if they paid the jizya and submitted to the other restrictions of *dhimmi* status.

The Hindus whom the invaders encountered in Sindh were not "people of the book." Accordingly, they had no option to submit to Islamic rule; they had either to convert to Islam or they would be killed. Muhammad ibn Qasim's overlord, Iraqi governor Hajjaj ibn Yusuf, instructed him to be ruthless: "My ruling is given: Kill anyone belonging to the combatants [*ahl-i harb*]; arrest their sons and daughters for hostages and imprison them."[53]

Yet in practice, this proved unworkable. There were simply too many Hindus for all of them either to be converted or killed. Muhammad ibn Qasim ultimately decided to grant Hindus "people of the book" status, despite their having no such book. This allowed the jizya to be collected from them, aiding the growth and prosperity of Muslim rule in India.[54]

As Muslim fortunes waxed and waned in India, the jizya was not collected for considerable periods, but began to be collected systematically during the reign of Firoz Shah Tughlaq, the Sultan of Delhi from 1351 to 1388. With the Hindus providing a steady source of income, the Islamic domains continued to expand, particularly after the Mughals conquered and absorbed the Sultanate of Delhi.

After two centuries of increasing dominance, Akbar the Great became Mughal emperor in 1556. Unlike all the other Muslim rulers of India both before and after him, Akbar became disenchanted with Islam, which ultimately led him to abolish the jizya.[55] His reforms, however, did not last—even his son and successor Jahangir did not continue them—but the jizya continued to be collected only intermittently until 1679, when the

---

[53] Derryl N. MacLean, Religion and Society in Arab Sind (Leiden: Brill, 1989), 37.

[54] K. S. Lal, The Legacy of Muslim Rule in India (New Delhi: Aditya Prakashan, 1992), 118.

[55] Hermann Kulke and Dietmar Rothermund, A History of India (Oxfordshire: Routledge, 2016), 361; Smith, The Oxford History of India, op. cit., 350.

notorious Mughal emperor Aurangzeb restored it throughout his domains.

The eighteenth-century Muslim history *Kanzu i-Mahfuz* states that Mughal emperors had for many years collected a fee from Hindu pilgrims to a popular temple in the city of Agra. Aurangzeb, however, had a broader system of taxation in mind. He ordered the temple in Agra destroyed, explaining to his noblemen that there was a better way to get revenue for the state: "I have considered well on the subject, and have reflected on it deeply; but if you wish to augment the revenue, there is a better plan for attaining the object by exacting the *jizya*. By this means, idolatry will be suppressed, the Muhammadan religion and the true faith will be honored, our proper duty will be performed, the finances of the state will be increased, and the infidels will be disgraced."[56]

The finances of the state were not increased for long. Aurangzeb's son Bahadur Shah abolished the *jizya* again early in the eighteenth century, and this time it was not restored. Without Hindus providing a steady source of revenue, the Mughal state began to go into rapid decline, beset by internal dissension and external threats. In the late eighteenth century, the British arrived, and began to expand their control until they had established the entire subcontinent as a British colony.

Just as in the case of the Ottoman Empire, the Mughal Empire began to crumble after the jizya was definitively abolished. Both empires had prospered when there was a substantial and generally wealthy captive population of non-Muslims who could finance further imperial expansion and the prosperity of the imperial

56 Arun Shourie, Harsh Narain, Jay Dubashi, Ram Swarup, and Sita Ram Goel, Hindu Temples: What Happened to Them, vol. 1, A Preliminary Survey (New Delhi: Voice of India, 1990), 288; Vincent Arthur Smith, The Oxford History of India: From the Earliest Times to the End of 1911 (Oxford: Clarendon Press, 1920), 438.

domains at large. Once this was no longer the case Islam's culture offered no other pathway to societal health and prosperity. Without the *jizya*, the Islamic domains were doomed.

A PARASITICAL CULTURE

In Iran, the primary source of *jizya* payments were the Zoroastrians—the people who held to the ancient religion of Persia that Islam had violently supplanted. The *jizya* was finally abolished there in 1882, when a group based in India—the Persian Zoroastrian Amelioration Fund—successfully pressured the government of Naser al-Din Shah Qajar to ease the persecution of this long-suffering people. By that time, however, the Zoroastrians had been reduced to a minuscule minority, unable to provide any significant financing for the Islamic state, and Iran was, not coincidentally, by this time an economic backwater.

In the 1930s, Reza Shah, who was Shah of Iran from 1925 to 1941, saw what Kemal Ataturk had done in Turkey and strove to emulate it in Iran as much as circumstances in his country would allow. He required Iranian men to adopt Western dress, and even dared to allow his wife and daughters to appear in public without wearing the Islamic veil. He explained, "The women of our country, because of their exclusion from society, have been unable to display their talent and ability. I might say they have been unable to do their duty toward their beloved country and people."[57]

The shah didn't mention that they had been excluded from society because of Islam, but everyone in Iran knew that already. Journalist Elaine Sciolino writes tactfully that Reza Shah "believed

---

[57] James Buchan, Days of God: The Revolution In Iran and Its Consequences (New York: Simon & Schuster, 2012), 34.

that many of Iran's problems stemmed from 'Arabization' and used his reign to distance Iran from the Arabs."[58] And while there is no doubt that Iran—which has a history and culture much longer and richer than that of any Arab nation—has sometimes chafed under the strictures of its adoptive Arab supremacist religion, Reza Shah was also unmistakably targeting Islam; he just couldn't be as forthright about that aspect of his program.

What Kemal Ataturk and Reza Shah may have seen as Islam's corrosive effect on a society was its parasitical nature. Islam could not provide that sustainable foundation for the very same reason that the Ottoman Empire initially prospered and then went into an irreversible decline. As proud Islamic warriors, mundane pursuits such as operating businesses or farms were beneath them. They lived off the taxes they collected from the subject peoples, and when those communities were bled dry, the empire was unable to sustain its previous level of prosperity because its own people had no work ethic. They worked if they had to for survival, but as Weber noted, unlike Protestants in Northern Europe, Muslims didn't believe that work could be a source of divine blessings rather than an onerous necessity that was required only when the despised conquered people provided insufficient income. The relationship of the Ottomans and Mughals to their dhimmi communities was one of a parasite to its hosts. When those hosts began to fall into poverty, the parasite did as well.

This pattern has been replicated everywhere that Islam has been implemented. Until relatively recently, the primary source of income for Islamic states has been—aside from the geological accident of striking it rich with fossil fuels—the money it could

58 Elaine Sciolino, Persian Mirrors: The Elusive Face of Iran (New York: Free Press, 2000), 170.

seize from conquered people in *jizya* payments. This required constant jihad to keep on expanding Islamic polities, or else they would face the same decline and ultimate destruction that was the fate of the Ottomans.

THE DEATH OF THE *JIZYA*

The Ottomans abolished the *dhimma* under Western pressure in the 1850s, and jizya is not collected today in any of the countries that once formed part of the Ottoman Empire, or in any other majority-Muslim countries. One key reason is because they do not consider themselves to be caliphates—states ruled by someone who styles himself the successor of Muhammad. Even Saudi Arabia, the Kingdom of the Two Holy Places, does not collect the jizya. Non-Muslim religious practice is forbidden inside the kingdom, so there would be no one from whom to collect it. If the Saudis decided to collect it from Christian and Hindu guest workers, it might find its steady labor supply from the poor countries that supply them drying up. Saudi Arabia has been so fantastically wealthy—because of an accident of geology, the discovery of oil—that collection of the *jizya* has not even been suggested.

Nonetheless, dhimmitude and the collection of the *jizya* remain part of Islamic law and the ideal Islamic state would still collect the *jizya* from those it had reduced to dhimmitude. During the Islamic State's short-lived caliphate in Iraq and Syria in the late 2010s, its jihadis once again collected it from Christians who were unfortunate enough to find themselves living within its domains.

Occasionally members of other Muslim groups say it should once again be collected. In 2014, a Sunni Muslim cleric in Saudi Arabia recommended that Sunni-majority nations collect it from

Shi'ite Muslims.[59] That same year, Yunis al-Astal, a Muslim cleric who was also a member of the Palestinian Legislative Council for Hamas, said of the Jews, "We must restore them to the state of humiliation imposed upon them. They should be dhimmi citizens. This status must be imposed upon them by war. They must pay the *jizya* security tax while they live in our midst.... However, in Palestine, where they are occupiers and invaders, they cannot have the status of dhimmis."[60]

If Salah, Nuseirat, and other Muslims who believe that Islam is the solution for what ails the nation get their wish for an Islamized America, it would likely be another parasitical state like the Ottoman or Mughal Empire. An Islamic America would almost certainly still have a substantial non-Muslim population, even if there were mass conversions to Islam. This might make for some initial prosperity and strength of the state, but as the non-Muslim communities grew smaller and weaker, the state itself would weaken as well.

DISENCHANTMENT IN IRAN

Is the solution for America really a political and social system that will impoverish it? One that will result in the subjugation of women and non-Muslims, and the destruction of lives for Sharia crimes such as blasphemy and apostasy? The wreckage of Islamic societies lies all around us. The Islamic Republic of Iran—arguably the most consistent state in the world today regarding its

59 "A Saudi Cleric Requests Jizya from Shia Muslims!!!," Shia Rights Watch, January 8, 2014, https://shiarightswatch.org/a-saudi-cleric-requests-jizya-from-shia-muslims/. Accessed October 30, 2024.

60 "Hamas MP Al-Astal: We Must Massacre Jews, Impose Jizya Poll Tax on Them," MEMRI, March 6, 2014, https://www.memri.org/tv/hamas-mp-al-astal-we-must-massacre-jews-impose-jizya-poll-tax-them. Accessed October 30, 2024.

uncompromising and unequivocal implementation of Sharia norms—is not only an economic basket case with a GNI lower than those of Pakistan, Vietnam, and Bangladesh, but a deeply unpopular regime that is in a state of more or less constant war against its own people, regularly applying the Qur'anic directive to "strike terror in the enemies of Allah" (8:60) in order to maintain power.

Islamic rule, in fact, has led to widespread disenchantment with Islam in Iran. In June 2020, a research organization, the Group for Analyzing and Measuring Attitudes in IRAN (GAMAAN), conducted an anonymous online survey on religious views in Iran after forty years of Islamic rule. Nearly 40,000 Iranians participated. The survey organizers reported "dramatic changes in Iranian religiosity, with an increase in secularisation and a diversity of faiths and beliefs."[61] While Iran is officially over 99 percent Muslim, only forty percent of the Iranians who participated in this anonymous survey said that they were Muslim. Nine percent said they were atheists, eight percent were Zoroastrians, and 1.5 percent said that they were Christian.

This was an extraordinary decline from a near-unanimous commitment to Islam that had persisted for centuries. After forty years of strict Islamic rule, Iranians were so far from thinking that it was the solution for society's ills that massive numbers of them didn't identify as Muslim at all.

It may seem strange to say that a religion is a failure. Muslims will insist that this cannot possibly be known for sure until the next world, when the unbelievers will weep bitter tears of

---

[61] Pooyan Tamimi Arab and Ammar Maleki, "Iran's secular shift: new survey reveals huge changes in religious beliefs," The Conversation, September 10, 2020, https://theconversation.com/irans-secular-shift-new-survey-reveals-huge-changes-in-religious-beliefs-145253. Accessed October 30, 2024.

regret for not recognizing the prophethood of Muhammad and embracing Islam. The religion of Muhammad, however, makes certain claims about the rewards of the believer in this world. The Qur'an says: "Allah has promised those of you who believe and do good works that he will surely make them succeed on the earth even as he caused those who were before them to succeed, and that he will surely establish for them their religion which he has approved for them, and will give them in exchange safety after their fear." (24:55)

This promise has not been kept. The believers in Allah have not succeeded on this earth, nor has their failure been disconnected from their religion. Islam is responsible for the economic failure of majority Muslim states, and for the lowly status of women and non-Muslims within them. Historian and sociologist Hugh Fitzgerald has noted that their "inshallah-fatalism" and lack of a work ethic condemn Islamic societies to poverty everywhere, for the *jizya* is not currently collected, even in countries where non-Muslim communities suffer considerable institutionalized discrimination and harassment, such as Pakistan, Indonesia, and Egypt.

CHAPTER FOUR
DESTROYING THE BELOVED

Despite Islam's manifest failure, its love/hate relationship with the West continues, and has more than once manifested itself in the confidence that one day Muslims would fully possess the "beloved,"—the hated enemy. Muslim leaders have for years made no secret of their certainty that the West's conquest and Islamization were imminent.

In 2005, the new president of the Islamic Republic of Iran, Mahmoud Ahmadinejad, said: "Have no doubt.... Allah willing, Islam will conquer what? It will conquer all the mountain tops of the world."[62] The whole world, yes, but the focus was on the West. In 2002, the world-renowned Muslim cleric Sheikh Yusuf al-Qaradawi declared: "Islam will return to Europe as a conqueror and victor, after being expelled from it twice."[63]

---

62 "Iran's New President Glorifies Martyrdom," MEMRI, July 29, 2005, https://www.memri.org/reports/irans-new-president-glorifies-martyrdom. Accessed October 30, 2024.

63 "Leading Sunni Sheikh Yousef Al-Qaradhawi and Other Sheikhs Herald the Coming Conquest of Rome," MEMRI, December 6, 2002, https://www.memri.org/reports/leading-sunni-sheikh-yousef-al-qaradhawi-and-other-sheikhs-herald-coming-conquest-rome. Accessed October 30, 2024.

Dr. Tareq al-Suwaidan, an Islamic scholar and Muslim Brotherhood leader based in Kuwait, said in January 2024, "One of the promises of the Prophet [Muhammad] is that Judgement Day will not happen until Islam prevails and we become victorious and we will rule the whole world. It's up to you to believe or not. But the [Prophet Muhammad's] Companions truly believed, and I hope that we truly believe, not in geopolitics, but in the promise of the Prophet [Muhammad]."[64]

Muslims in the United States have said much the same. Omar Ahmad, the cofounder and longtime Board chairman of the Hamas-linked Council on American-Islamic Relations (CAIR), said, "Islam isn't in America to be equal to any other faith, but to become dominant. The Koran should be the highest authority in America, and Islam the only accepted religion on earth."[65] When these words were initially published in a news report, Ahmad denied saying them; however, the reporter who had been present when Ahmad spoke, Lisa Gardiner of the *Fremont Argus*, maintained that her story was accurate.[66]

Adding to the likelihood that Ahmad's words had indeed been reported accurately was a similar statement from longtime CAIR spokesman Ibrahim Hooper: "I wouldn't want to create

---

64 "Kuwaiti Islamic Scholar And Muslim Brotherhood Leader Dr. Tareq Al-Suwaidan: The Prophet Muhammad Promised Us That We Will Rule The Whole World; I Met Hamas Leader Haniyeh Last Week, He Said Hamas Lost Less Than 20% If Its Power, Is Prepared For A Long Battle That Will Destroy Israeli Society; The Palestinians Are Fighting The Greatest Empires Of The World, Who Support Israel," MEMRI, January 21, 2024, https://www.memri.org/tv/kuwaiti-muslim-brotherhood-leader-tareq-suwaidan-islam-will-rule-world. Accessed October 30, 2024.

65 Art Moore, "Did CAIR founder say Islam to rule America?," WorldNetDaily, December 11, 2006, https://www.wnd.com/2006/12/39229/. Accessed October 30, 2024.

66 Ibid.

the impression that I wouldn't like the government of the United States to be Islamic sometime in the future."[67]

In service of that goal, the Muslim Brotherhood says in a captured internal document that its goal in the United States is "eliminating and destroying Western civilization from within, and sabotaging its miserable house...so that it falls, and Allah's religion is victorious over other religions."[68]

In 2007, Abdul Alim Musa, an imam in Washington, DC, stated that as far as he was concerned, the goal of Muslims in America should be to "establish an Islamic State of America by 2050."[69]

One of America's best-known Muslim leaders and a highly sought-after figure on the Muslim speaking circuit, Siraj Wahhaj, said in 1992: "If only Muslims were clever politically, they could take over the United States and replace its constitutional government with a caliphate."[70]

These beliefs can have and have had lethal consequences. In January 2022, one of the most wanted terrorists in Kenya, Rashid Mohamed Salim, was captured in the Democratic Republic of the Congo. Salim was known to be particularly vicious, as one

---

67 Minneapolis Star Tribune, April 4, 1993, quoted in Daniel Pipes and Sharon Chadha, "CAIR: Islamists Fooling the Establishment," Middle East Quarterly, Spring 2006, https://www.meforum.org/middle-east-quarterly/cair-islamists-fooling-the-establishment. Accessed October 30, 2024.

68 Mohamed Akram, "An Explanatory Memorandum on the General Strategic Goal for the Group in North America," May 22, 1991, Government Exhibit 003-0085, US vs. HLF, et al. P. 7 (21), https://centerforsecuritypolicy.org/wp-content/uploads/2014/05/Explanatory_Memoradum.pdf. Accessed October 30, 2024.

69 Robert Spencer, "DC Imam wants to establish an 'Islamic State of North America no later than 2050,'" Jihad Watch, November 9, 2007, https://jihadwatch.org/2007/11/dc-imam-wants-to-establish-an-islamic-state-of-north-america-no-later-than-2050. Accessed October 24, 2024.

70 Laura L. Rubenfeld, "Democrats Embrace Siraj Wahhaj: Supporter of Cop-Killer, Al Qaeda and Hamas," FrontPageMagazine.com, August 29, 2012, https://www.meforum.org/islamist-watch/democrats-embrace-siraj-wahhaj-supporter-of-cop-37450. Accessed October 24, 2024.

person on the scene in the city of Beni recounted: "This young man is a great terrorist. He is a very big player in the activities of slaughtering Christians in this part of Beni. We have been receiving pictures and short films of him cutting the throats of Christians and the police. It is said that he is the one who captures them or has them captured via his telephone by fellow rebels when he is in the process of acting and publishes them as propaganda. He is already an Allied Democratic Forces (ADF) commander."[71] (The ADF, contrary to its name, was a jihad group aligned with the Islamic State.)

Salim in captivity was shown a video of himself beheading an officer of the Armed Forces of the Democratic Republic of the Congo (FARDC). He explained: "I was given a machete by the ADF rebels to behead the government's soldier that we had captured. They told me to draw attention to all the people of the world that there was Islam in Congo, and they were invited to come and spread the Islamic religion so that Islam can rule the whole world. So I killed the FARDC soldier in the name of Allah."[72]

NOT "EXTREMISM"

These men are not "extremists." They were articulating what is standard Islamic doctrine. The ninth-century biographer of Muhammad, Ibn Hisham, was the first to assert that while Islam's message was at first peaceful and tolerant, it ultimately became one of bloody conquest. Initially, according to Ibn Hisham,

71 "Kenya's Most Wanted Terrorist Arrested in the DRC," International Christian Concern, January 30, 2022, https://persecution.org/2022/01/30/kenyas-most-wanted-terrorist-arrested-in-the-drc/.

72 Ibid.

Muhammad "had not been given permission to fight or allowed to shed blood.... He had simply been ordered to call men to God and to endure insult and forgive the ignorant."[73] However, eventually Allah "gave permission to His apostle to fight and to protect himself against those who wronged them and treated them badly."[74] Then Allah revealed the command for offensive jihad: "Then God sent down to him: 'Fight them so that there be no more seduction,' i.e. until no believer is seduced from his religion. 'And the religion is God's', i.e. Until God alone is worshipped."[75] This was Qur'an 2:193 and 8:39, which commanded Muslims to fight until "the religion is all for Allah."[76]

A chief justice of Saudi Arabia, Sheikh Abdullah bin Muhammad ibn Humaid, agreed: "At first 'the fighting' was forbidden, then it was permitted and after that it was made obligatory."[77] So did Sayyid Qutb, who quoted the fourteenth-century Islamic theologian and jurist Ibn Qayyim, writing about Muhammad: "For thirteen years after the beginning of his Messengership, he called people to God through preaching, without fighting or *Jizyah*, and was commanded to restrain himself and to practice patience and forbearance. Then he was commanded to migrate, and later permission was given to fight. Then he was commanded to fight those who fought him, and to restrain himself from those who did not make war with him. Later he was

---

73 A. Guillaume, The Life of Muhammad: A Translation of Ibn Ishaq's Sirat Rasul Allah (Oxford: Oxford University Press, 1955), 212–213.

74 Ibid.

75 Ibid.

76 Ibid.

77 Abdullah bin Muhammad bin Humaid, "The Call to Jihad (Holy Fighting for Allah's Cause) in the Qur'an," Appendix III of Muhammed Ibn Ismaiel Al-Bukhari, Sahih al-Bukhari: The Translation of the Meanings, trans. Muhammad M. Khan (Riyadh: Darussalam, 1997), vol. 9, 462.

commanded to fight the polytheists until God's religion was fully established."[78]

Qutb offers his own summary of Ibn Qayyim's words: "Thus, according to the explanation by Imam Ibn Qayyim, the Muslims were first restrained from fighting; then they were permitted to fight; then they were commanded to fight against the aggressors; and finally they were commanded to fight against all the polytheists."[79]

Qutb quotes Ibn Qayyim further regarding the subjugation of non-Muslims: "It was also explained that war should be declared against those from among the 'People of the Book' who declare open enmity, until they agree to pay Jizyah or accept Islam. Concerning the polytheists and the hypocrites, it was commanded in this chapter that Jihaad be declared against them and that they be treated harshly."[80] Qutb adds if someone declines to accept Islam, "then it is the duty of Islam to fight him until either he is killed or until he declares his submission."[81]

The twelfth century Islamic jurist Ibn Rushd stated that "Muslim jurists agreed that the purpose of fighting with the People of the Book…is one of two things: it is either their conversion to Islam or the payment of *jizyah*."[82] Imran Ahsan Khan Nyazee, a twentieth-century professor of Sharia in Pakistan, emphasizes that this is not an ancient and discarded belief, but an obligation that Muslims today must take up: "This leaves no doubt that the primary goal of the Muslim community, in the eyes of its jurists, is to spread the word of Allah through jihad,

78 Qutb, Milestones, op. cit., 53.
79 Ibid., 64.
80 Ibid., 53–4.
81 Ibid., 57.
82 Imran Ahsan Khan Nyazee, Theories of Islamic Law: The Methodology of Ijtihad (Selangor, Malaysia: The Other Press, 1994) 251–2.

and the option of poll-tax [jizya] is to be exercised only after subjugation" of non-Muslims.[83]

The twenty-first century Saudi Islamic scholar Abu Bakr Jabir al-Jaza'iri explains in a similar vein that jihad involves "fighting against the disbelievers and those who wage war against Islam."[84] Once fought against and conquered, infidels will "respond to the Muslims by paying the Jizyah tax. It is a pact in which they promise the Muslims to adhere to the laws of Islamic Shari'ah related to the prescribed laws of punishment, such as for murder, stealing and breach of honor."[85] Non-Muslims are not permitted to labor in "constructing Churches or Synagogues, or renovating the demolished ones," or "erecting the residence of non-Muslims above the homes of the Muslims." They are likewise not permitted to consume pork or alcohol, or to eat or drink in public during Ramadan daylight hours.[86]

Al-Azhar University in Cairo, the most influential theological and legal institution in Sunni Islam, labels a manual of Islamic law as reflecting "the practice and faith of the orthodox Sunni community."[87] That manual states that the "lesser jihad" is "war against non-Muslims," while the greater jihad is the struggle against sin within the individual soul.[88] While violent jihad is "lesser," the legal manual is much more preoccupied with it than it is with the "greater jihad," and stipulates that "the caliph makes

---

83 Ibid.

84 Abu Bakr Jabir al-Jaza'iri, Minhaj al-Muslim: A Book of Creed, Manners, Character, Acts of Worship and Other Deeds (Riyadh: Darussalam, 2001), 165.

85 Ibid., 182.

86 Ibid., 184.

87 Ahmed ibn Naqib al-Misri, Reliance of the Traveller ('Umdat al-Salik): A Classic Manual of Islamic Sacred Law, trans. Nuh Ha Mim Keller (Beltsville, Maryland: Amana Publications, 1999), xx.

88 Ibid., o9.0.

war upon Jews, Christians, and Zoroastrians…until they become Muslim or pay the non-Muslim poll tax."[89]

This war may only begin once the caliph "has first invited [Jews, Christians, and Zoroastrians] to enter Islam in faith and practice, and if they will not, then invited them to enter the social *order* of Islam by paying the non-Muslim poll tax (jizya)…while remaining in their ancestral religions."[90] This is one of the reasons why Islamic jihad groups worldwide want to reestablish the caliphate. But the manual also says that if there is no caliph, Muslims must still wage jihad to defend Islam.[91]

In 1979, a Pakistani Brigadier, S. K. Malik, published a book entitled *The Qur'anic Concept of War*. In it, he explained that the Qur'anic teaching regarding warfare against unbelievers underwent an evolution, with war for conquest being the last and permanent stage: "The Muslim migration to Medina brought in its wake events and decisions of far-reaching significance and consequence for them. While in Mecca, they had neither been proclaimed an Ummah [community] nor were they granted the permission to take up arms against their oppressors. In Medina, a divine revelation proclaimed them an 'Ummah' and granted them the permission to take up arms against their oppressors. The permission was soon afterwards converted into a divine command making war a religious obligation for the faithful."[92]

The twentieth-century Islamic legal scholar Majid Khadduri explained, "The Islamic state, whose principal function was to put God's law into practice, sought to establish Islam as the dominant reigning ideology over the entire world.… The jihad was

89 Ibid., o9.8.
90 Ibid.
91 Ibid., o9.6.
92 S. K. Malik, The Qur'anic Concept of War (Delhi: Adam Publishers, 1992), 11.

therefore employed as an instrument for both the universalization of religion and the establishment of an imperial world state."[93]

UNIVERSALIZATION AND DOMINANCE

Khadduri's summation is apt: the jihad is waged in order to establish Islam as the world's "dominant reigning ideology," and to bring about the "universalization of religion." These are Qur'anic imperatives, based on the Muslims' obligation to fight until "religion is all for Allah" (8:39, 2:193) and to establish the hegemony of the "best of people" (3:110) over the "most vile of created beings" (98:6). When Allah bestows the title of "best of people" upon the Muslims, he adds, "You command what is right and forbid what is wrong, and you believe in Allah." (3:110) It is thus because of their belief in Islam and their knowledge of Sharia, Allah's perfect law that sets forth what is right and what is wrong, that Muslims are the best of people. If they stop adhering to Sharia and trying to impose it upon the infidels, then they lose their status as the best of people and become hypocrites, who are frequently excoriated throughout the Qur'an.

Consequently, it's not enough for Muslims to conquer non-Muslim lands and subjugate the non-Muslims. "Islam must dominate and is not to be dominated," said the founder of the Muslim Brotherhood, Hasan al-Banna,[94] because this dominance demonstrates most vividly that the Muslims are indeed "the best of people." Coexistence is not possible, for how can the "best of people" live as equals with "the most vile of created beings"?

---

93 Majid Khadduri, War and Peace in the Law of Islam (Baltimore: Johns Hopkins University Press, 1955), 51.

94 "Hasan al-Banna," Encyclopedia of the Middle East, MidEastWeb, http://www.mideast-web.org/Middle-East-Encyclopedia/hassan_al-banna.htm. Accessed October 24, 2024.

This imperative to dominate also explains why so many sacred sites around the world are objects of dispute between Muslims and people of other religions. Muslims claim, as sacred to Islam, the site of the ancient Jewish Temple in Jerusalem, and—just as the Islamic religion was being formulated—constructed two mosques, the Al-Aqsa Mosque and the Dome of the Rock, on the Temple Mount. People today generally take for granted that the Temple Mount is a disputed site, but rarely does anyone consider why it is so.

The site has been sacred to the Jews since time immemorial, while only late in the seventh century were the mosques built there, and only in the ninth century was the story of Muhammad's miraculous night journey to Jerusalem and ascension into paradise from the Temple Mount—during which ascent he met the other prophets and conversed with Allah himself—finally committed to writing, or more likely, finally formulated as a justification for the Muslims' claim to Jerusalem as a city holy to Islam.

One may consider it a remarkable coincidence that the site of the destroyed Jewish Temple—a site always much revered among Jews—would be exactly the same place from which Allah chose to bring Muhammad into paradise, but it is actually no coincidence at all. The two mosques are on the Temple Mount precisely because the Jewish Temple had been there. The presence of the mosques is meant to show the victory of Islam over Judaism, and its superiority to the older religion. It is meant to show that Islam is now the "dominant reigning ideology."

9/11 hijacker Mohamed Atta reminded himself to "shout, 'Allahu Akbar,' because this strikes fear in the hearts of the non-believers."[95] Terror, however, was not the sole objective. "Allahu akbar" means "Allah is greater," not "God is great," as Western media outlets often translate it. Jihadis scream "Allahu akbar" as they carry out their attacks to assert that Allah is greater than the god in whom the jihadi's victim believes. Screams of "Allahu akbar" so often accompany violence and destruction, because Allah's superiority is shown in the victimization of the infidels, whom Allah said would suffer in this world as well as in the next, and in the destruction or appropriation of the infidels' holy sites. "Just travel in the land," says the Qur'an, "and see the nature of the consequences for those who denied" (3:137)—that is, denied that there was no god but Allah and Muhammad was his prophet. The destruction of the sacred sites of non-Muslims, or their repurposing as mosques, bore mute witness to Allah's punishment of the unbelievers, and of the triumph of Islam.

The Temple Mount is not unique; this is seen everywhere Islam has conquered. In Constantinople—for over a thousand years the capital of the Roman Empire—Hagia Sophia cathedral stood for nine hundred of those years as the grandest church in the Christian world, the crown jewel of the city that was the capital of the Christian empire. On May 29, 1453, when Constantinople finally fell to the warriors of Islam after a lengthy siege (and nearly eight hundred years of other attempts), one of the first acts of the Ottoman Sultan Mehmed the Conqueror was to make his way to Hagia Sophia, where he had a muezzin mount the pulpit and proclaim that there was no god but Allah, and Muhammad was his prophet. The Great Church was now a mosque. Numerous other churches were converted to mosques as well.

---

95 "Last words of a terrorist," The Guardian, September 30, 2001, https://www.theguardian.com/world/2001/sep/30/terrorism.september113. Accessed October 30, 2024.

Why couldn't the conquerors have left the Christians their churches and built mosques elsewhere? Much later, after the British and French conquered Muslim lands in the Middle East, North Africa, and Central Asia, the Christians behaved in exactly that way toward the Muslims in their colonial domains. For all the opprobrium that is heaped upon Western colonialism these days, Western colonial governments taking action to restrict Islam in any way, or to harm Muslims, are rare to the point of nonexistent.

The colonialist imperative that Mehmed the Conqueror represents, in contrast, was much more thoroughgoing. Following the pattern of centuries of jihad conquests before him, Mehmed determinedly and unapologetically seized the sites that the conquered people held most sacred, and imposed the *jizya* upon the Jews and Christians of his new domains in order to give them a ready inducement to convert to Islam. Yet for all that, Islamic conquests aren't even recognized today as a kind of colonialism; only the children and heirs of those who practiced the West's much gentler form of colonialism must bear shame for doing so.

Nevertheless, Mehmed's transformation of Hagia Sophia into a mosque was colonialism *par excellence*; more than that, it was another mute but unmistakable declaration that demonstrated the victory of Islam over Christianity, and the superiority of the younger faith to the older one.

The same pattern played out all over India, as the Muslim conquerors destroyed thousands of Hindu temples and built mosques atop their ruins. Once again, another site would not do. To build a mosque across town from a Hindu temple would not demonstrate the victory and superiority of Islam. Only destruction of the Hindu worship spaces would accomplish that.

Yet all these proclamations of Islam's supremacy have a hollow ring in light of the fact that, while the military superiority of the forces of Islam at various points throughout history has been unquestionable, that superiority has only partially and infrequently manifested itself in other areas.

Islam is condemned forever to define itself only in terms of its relationships with competing faiths, rather than on its own terms. Islam is superior because it has conquered Jerusalem, Constantinople, and Ayodhya, and so many other places, and established visible signs of its superiority at the expense of the infidels. No other religion, however, feels the need to define itself solely in terms of having bested others on the battlefield or in other ways. There are polemical writings among followers of all religions, and criticism of the various religions, but all other religions can exist perfectly well without having to show that they're superior at the expense of others. Only Islam must do that.

CHAPTER FIVE

FAILURE BREEDS JIHAD

THE REMEDY: MORE ISLAM

Many people, both Muslim and non-Muslim, have noticed Islam has failed in its quest to dominate the world, but few have been willing to admit it for what it is. Instead, the formulation of excuses for this failure has become a venerable tradition in Islam, and a veritable cottage industry in our own day.

The foremost excuse is fraught with dangers for unbelievers.

"Allah, The All-Knower," says the Muslim question-and-answer site IslamWeb.net, "has informed us that the good deeds are a means to living a good life now and being rewarded by Paradise on the Day of Judgement."[96] It offers a proof text from the Qur'an in support of this idea: "Whoever does righteousness, whether male or female, while he is a believer—We will surely cause him to live a good life, and We will surely give them their reward

---

96 "Success in this world," IslamWeb.net, https://www.islamweb.net/en/fatwa/82910/success-in-this-world. Accessed August 28, 2024.

[in the Hereafter] according to the best of what they used to do." (16:97)[97]

IslamWeb goes on to emphasize that this promise goes for both this world and the next: "So anyone who wants to be happy in this worldly life and the Hereafter should stick firmly to the Quran and the Sunnah and abide by what is in them, performing the orders and avoiding the prohibited matters.... So, anybody who embodies the attributes mentioned in these verses will be successful in this worldly life and the Hereafter. He will live honorably and die honorably."[98]

This promise comes with a warning: "this Ummah will not evolve from its sleepiness nor will it obtain victory in its battles, nor will it get the mastery of the world unless it applies the Sharee'ah of Allah as explained in the Quran and the Sunnah in all the fields of life."[99] The success of the Muslims in this world depended upon their adherence to Sharia principles: "When the Muslims were applying the religion in all the fields of life, Allah gave them victory over all other people and made them a cause for the guidance of many people. All people on the earth recognized the rule of Muslims and their enemies testified to their justice and good behavior."[100]

The author of this fatwa is sure that the ills of the global Muslim community in the present day stem from its laxity in obeying all the commands of Allah: "Now the state of the Muslim Ummah will not change to the best unless it applies what the good processors applied. In fact, the present life of this Ummah will not be good except by what made it good in its past. To do

---

97 Ibid.
98 Ibid.
99 Ibid.
100 Ibid.

otherwise, the Ummah can only expect a humiliation that Allah will not lift until it returns to His Religion."[101]

The remedy for the ills of the Islamic world, in this view, couldn't possibly be simpler: return to Islam. Obey Allah, and you will prosper. Disobey Allah, and you will suffer. This is a vastly different spiritual landscape from that of the Judeo-Christian tradition, which is frequently preoccupied with the question of why the unrighteous so often do so well in this life. Job complains, "Why do the wicked live, reach old age, and grow mighty in power?" (Job 21:7) The psalmist admits: "For I was envious of the arrogant, when I saw the prosperity of the wicked." (Psalm 73:3) "Why does the way of the wicked prosper?," asks the prophet Jeremiah. "Why do all who are treacherous thrive?" (Jeremiah 12:1).

Such questions are rare in the Islamic tradition. Allah does what he wills. One should not be too inquisitive about such matters, for "A people before you asked, and then became unbelievers." (Qur'an 5:102) Allah promises that those who obey him will find success both in this world and the next, and that's the end of the matter. If someone encounters difficulty in life, it is because he is unrighteous, and his sins have displeased Allah. The idea of righteous Job, suffering unjustly despite the cleanness of his heart, is alien to Islam.

This view of the world creates breeding grounds for violent fanaticism in many Muslim countries. This is because of the central role of jihad in Islamic thought. A hadith depicts Muhammad being asked, "Instruct me as to such a deed as equals Jihad (in reward)." He answers: "I do not find such a deed."[102] In another

---

101 Ibid.

102 Bukhari, vol. 4, book 56, no. 2785, https://sunnah.com/bukhari:2785. Accessed October 30, 2024.

hadith Muhammad says that "a single endeavor (of fighting) in Allah's Cause in the forenoon or in the afternoon is better than the world and whatever is in it."[103] There is nothing better that one can do than wage jihad.

If there is no deed that surpasses jihad in reward, and fighting in Allah's cause is greater than everything else in the world, then the failure in Islamic societies will breed jihadis. Islamic societies will seek to turn away Allah's wrath from their people by encouraging them to undertake the greatest deed of all in Islam: warfare against unbelievers. When nations suffer natural disasters or fall into poverty, Islamic preachers seize the disaster as an opportunity to call people back to the pure and wholehearted service of Allah, who will then prosper their works both in this world and in the next. Since jihad is the deed that Allah rewards most lavishly, it is also the most likely activity to reverse a downturn in fortunes.

HYPOCRITES OR TRUE BELIEVERS?

We can see this in microcosm in the lives of individual jihadis. In Paris on November 13, 2015, Islamic jihadis murdered 130 people and injured nearly 500 in attacks at the Bataclan theatre, where a rock concert was going on, as well as at other locations the same night. Footage later emerged of two of the principal jihadis responsible for that mass murder, Salah Abdeslam and his brother Brahim, dancing at a Brussels nightclub several months before the attacks. The UK's *Daily Mail*, always determined to ignore the jihadi mindset and motivations, misrepresenting both as quite other than what they are, took this as another indication

[103] Bukhari, vol. 4, book 56, no. 2792, https://sunnah.com/bukhari:2792. Accessed October 30, 2024.

that jihadis in general are not what they claim to be: "Video shows the extremists eight months before the massacre in Paris, seemingly enjoying the Westernised lifestyle ISIS claims to despise."[104] As always, however, reality is different from the establishment media's presentation of it.

Were the Abdeslam brothers hypocrites, and not true believers in Islam? There is no reason to assume this. The phenomenon of violent jihadis, apparently deeply committed to Islam yet engaging in un-Islamic behavior, was also seen in the run-up to the September 11, 2001, jihad attacks in New York and Washington. Shortly after nearly three thousand people were murdered in those attacks, it came to light that one of the principal 9/11 hijackers, Mohamed Atta, and several of his fellow jihadis, had been at a strip club not long before the attacks.

We were told, and have been told many times since, that—contrary to their own claims—this indicated that jihad terrorists are not pious Muslims acting upon the exhortations in the Qur'an and Sunnah to make war against unbelievers. On the contrary, goes this claim, these terrorists have nothing whatsoever to do with Islam, and are simply reacting to the alleged evils of the West. What pious, believing Muslim engaged in an act of jihad would risk sullying his soul in a strip club and thereby detracting from the spiritual value of his jihad?

This question, however, betrays in itself a lack of understanding of Islamic theology—a lack of understanding that continues, all these years after 9/11, to hamstring our response to the jihad threat. What is understood by precious few counter-terror

[104] Julian Robinson, "Murderers on the dance floor: Terror brothers filmed in Brussels nightclub months before Paris attacks…even though they were already becoming radicalized," Daily Mail, March 28, 2016, https://www.dailymail.co.uk/news/article-3512419/Murderers-dance-floor-Terror-brothers-filmed-Brussels-nightclub-months-Paris-attacks-radicalised.html. Accessed October 30, 2024.

analysts is that a pious, believing Muslim who is about to engage in a momentous act of jihad may very well engage in activity that Islamic law would deem sinful, and do so freely and knowingly.

The reasons for this are set out in the Qur'an and Hadith. The Qur'an teaches that if one's good deeds outweigh one's bad deeds on the great cosmic scales of justice, one will enter Paradise: "And we set a just balance for the day of resurrection so that no soul is wronged in anything. Even if it is the weight of a grain of mustard seed, we bring it. And we are sufficient as reckoners." (21:47) When one's deeds are weighed in these scales, the weightiest deed of all, as Muhammad himself explained, is waging jihad for the sake of Allah.

In light of all this, Salah and Brahim Abdeslam may well have known that they were going to commit jihad mass murder when they went dancing in Brussels several months before their killing spree. If they had been planning at that point to go killing for Allah in jihad, they could enjoy a night out and even a beer or two, knowing that the sinfulness of it all would be far outweighed by their jihad.

Friends of the brothers recount, however, that their turn to Islam came after the night out captured on video: "I saw Salah joke, smoke, drink and play cards. If anything, he liked women. He was something of a ladies' man and I heard he had a girlfriend at one point."[105] However, "that was the last time I saw them drink. Brahim started to become more religious. He would attend Friday prayers at the mosque but otherwise pray at home."[106]

---

105 Ibid.

106 Ibid.

Whether the jihad brothers actually became more religious after this night out, or were already in the process of doing so, we see another often denied, but frequently recurring phenomenonis: Muslims becoming devout in their observance of Islam and then becoming jihad murderers. And when they killed all those infidels in Paris, the Abdeslam brothers could be sure that whatever sins they had committed that night in Brussels—and any other nights that hadn't been captured on video—were far outweighed on Allah's scales of judgment by the blood of 130 non-Muslims killed for his cause. Their place in paradise was secured.

Salah Abdeslam was accordingly serene when he appeared in court in February 2018. Sitting between two special forces officers wearing balaclavas to conceal their identities from Abdeslam's fellow jihadis and holding machine guns should he or his friends attempt to mount another jihad attack right in the courtroom, he told a judge at the Palais de Justice in Brussels, "Judge me, do what you want with me, it's in my Lord that I place my trust. I am not afraid of you, I am not afraid of your allies. I put my trust in Allah and that's all, I have nothing else to add."[107] Yet he did add one more detail: "I declare that there is no god but Allah, Muhammad is his servant and his messenger."[108] Having carried out his jihad, Abdeslam could now be certain that his good deeds outweighed his bad deeds, and he would not suffer in hell no matter how far from Allah he might have strayed before he participated in the jihad massacre in Paris. That surpassed everything else.

---

107 "Paris terror suspect tells court: 'I am not afraid of you,'" Sky News, February 6, 2018, https://news.sky.com/story/paris-terror-suspect-tells-court-i-am-not-afraid-of-you-11237720. Accessed October 30, 2024.

108 Ibid.

The same fanaticism in pursuit of Allah's blessings can overtake societies as a whole. In October 2023, Pakistani journalist Muhammad Khurshid analyzed his country's political, social, and economic situation, explaining first that "a state, as defined by political science, comprises four essential components: territory, people, sovereignty, and government."[109] He found Pakistan to be severely lacking in all four. Its "territorial integrity remains intact, but its governance within this territory is in disarray."[110] Its people, meanwhile, "who should be the cornerstone of the state, are increasingly disillusioned with the government. The mismanagement of resources, economic hardships, and a lack of essential services have left them frustrated and disheartened."[111]

And while "true sovereignty lies with the people," in the case of Pakistan "it appears to have been hijacked by a select few who use the state's resources for personal gain."[112] Related to that problem was his assertion that the government, "designed to serve and protect the interests of the people, is often perceived as a tool for suppressing political opponents and dissent. This misuse of power has shaken the very foundations of democracy."[113]

Echoing Sayyid Qutb, Khurshid concluded, "It is evident that Pakistan's current democratic system has faltered, and the people's faith in the government has eroded. However, the solution lies in embracing the principles of Islam to establish a just, accountable, and prosperous society."[114] He asserted that "a system of governance inspired by the teachings of Islam" would "transform

---

109 Muhammad Khurshid, "Rethinking Governance in Pakistan: A Call for a Return to the Principles of Islam," LinkedIn, October 21, 2023. https://www.linkedin.com/pulse/rethinking-governance-pakistan-call-return-principles-khurshid/ Accessed September 2, 2024.

110 Ibid.

111 Ibid.

112 Ibid.

113 Ibid.

114 Ibid.

Pakistan from a state of turmoil into a peaceful and prosperous nation."[115] And so Pakistan has sought prosperity in adherence to Islam. In a 2013 report, the United States Institute of Peace described how deeply embedded Sharia-adherent, jihadist Islam, which it termed "extremism," had become in Pakistani society:

> The emotional resonance that extremists manage to generate in their Pakistani audiences has roots in the narratives that were developed and deployed in the establishment of Pakistan and in subsequent historical events. In Pakistan, globally oriented Islamist extremists have a population of 180 million that has been exposed to the main elements of extremist narratives for over six decades. Various extremist actors have exploited this situation to present an extremist rhetorical vision that is perceived as being analogous to the country's self-image. Al-Qaeda, as the world's most ambitious and arguably most successful Islamist extremist organization, has subsumed Pakistan's narratives into its own. In doing so, it is has succeeded in making the country seem like an international poster child for the extremist cause. Meanwhile, al-Qaeda's narratives have begun to form Pakistanis' views of the wider world.[116]

[115] Ibid.

[116] Amil Khan, "Pakistan and the Narratives of Extremism," United States Institute of Peace, Special Report 327, March 2013. https://www.usip.org/sites/default/files/SR327-Pakistan-and-the-Narratives-of-Extremism.pdf. Accessed September 2, 2024.

Yet in becoming "an international poster child" for the global jihad, out of the firm conviction that by doing so, it was demonstrating fidelity to Allah, Pakistan has become neither peaceful nor prosperous. A vicious cycle is thus created. Although piety, including jihadist sentiments, are inculcated in the population, still Allah's blessings remain elusive. The god who promised his blessings in this world as well as the next is unmoved by Pakistan's commitment to Islam, which indicates to the true believers that they still haven't attained a level of adherence to the religion that Allah would find acceptable. Thus they become even more fanatical than they were before, and that includes jihad as the greatest deed a human being can commit. If the nation still doesn't prosper, the only remedy is still more Islam.

This leads to the peculiar phenomenon that Pakistan, although it is one of the most scrupulously Sharia-adherent societies on earth, is also replete with Islamic groups that decry the nation's present unforgivable state of irreligion and demand even more Sharia adherence. A telling example of this came in February 2024, when Qazi Faez Isa, the Chief Justice of Pakistan's Supreme Court, issued a ruling regarding the right of Ahmadiyya community to publish and distribute its own commentary on the Qur'an. An Ahmadi, Mubarak Ahmed Sami, had been arrested in January 2023 for distributing the commentary, and charged with violating a 2021 law prohibiting the dissemination of "heterodox" Qur'an commentaries.[117]

In his defense, Sami insisted that he had only distributed the commentary in 2019, before the law was passed. Isa ruled in

---

117 Massimo Introvigne, "Pakistan, Council of Islamic Ideology Asks for Even Harsher Persecution of the Ahmadis," Bitter Winter, August 20, 2024, https://bitterwinter.org/pakistan-council-of-islamic-ideology-asks-for-even-harsher-persecution-of-the-ahmadis/. Accessed October 30, 2024.

his favor, saying that laws could not be retroactively applied, but did not challenge the law prohibiting the publication of Ahmadi texts. The Council of Islamic Ideology, an official government organization, was not satisfied with this, and took issue in particular with a statement in Isa's ruling that said Ahmadis were not permitted to express their faith "outside of their places of worship."[118] Even that was not enough for the Council, which declared that Ahmadis "must not be allowed to profess or preach in any manner even within their houses, community centers or in places of worship.... They must not be permitted to profess or preach openly, inside their houses or otherwise, as their actions directly desecrate the teachings of Prophet Muhammad (PBUH), Islam, the Quran, and the Sunnah. They should be unequivocally declared as apostates."[119]

The Ahmadiyya community could thus expect more violence from people who believed that, in terrorizing the Ahmadis, they would gain the divine favor for themselves and for the nation as a whole. Pakistan's failure led it to turn to jihad. And Pakistan's jihad made it a failure.

118 Ibid.

119 Ibid.

CHAPTER SIX

FAILURE BREEDS JEW-HATRED

THE CAUSE OF ALL THEIR TROUBLES

In the Qur'anic view of the world, the Jews are inveterate enemies of the Muslims, determined to deceive them, thwart their plans and cause them to fail. Thus when Islamic societies actually do fail, the Jews are the first to be blamed. This leads to the view that punishing the Jews with jihad attacks is a righteous act, restoring the natural order of things and putting the enemies of Allah in their place.

Another aspect of the natural order of things is that the Jews must be made to suffer in poverty and shame. This idea is clear from one of the Qur'an's many retellings of the Exodus story. Allah is depicted as telling the Children of Israel, "And we caused the white cloud to overshadow you and sent down the manna and the quails upon you. Eat of the good things with which we have provided you. They did not wrong us, but they did wrong themselves." (2:57) They did so by ungratefully demanding tastier fare than manna and quails: "And when you said, O Moses, we are weary of one kind of food, so call upon your Lord for us, that he would bring forth for us from what the earth grows, of its herbs and its cucumbers and its corn and its lentils and its onions. He said, Would you exchange what is higher for what is lower?" (2:61)

Ultimately, Moses has had enough, and tells his people: "Go down to a settled country, in this way you will get what you are demanding." (2:61) The complaining people get their expected punishment: "And humiliation and poverty struck them and they were visited with wrath from Allah. That was because they disbelieved in Allah's signs and killed the prophets wrongfully. That was for their disobedience and transgression." (2:61) Humiliation and poverty struck the Jews because of their disobedience.

Should one wish to avoid humiliation and poverty, then, one must avoid disobeying Allah. One must also be careful to shun the Jews, for "They will be stricken with disgrace wherever they are found, except for a rope from Allah and a rope from men. They have brought on anger from their Lord, and wretchedness is laid upon them. That is because they used to disbelieve the signs of Allah, and killed the prophets wrongfully. That is because they were rebellious and used to transgress." (3:112) The "rope from Allah" and "rope from men," according to a popular commentary on the Qur'an, refers to the non-Muslims' payment of the "atonement (Jizya) to the Muslim state, in which case they will be accorded the rights of a Dhimmi."[120]

The Qur'an's warning that the Jews "will be stricken with disgrace wherever they are found" follows closely after high praise for the Muslims: "You are the best of people that has been raised

120 Muhammad Aashiq Ilahi Bulandshahri, Illuminating Discourses on the Noble Qur'an (Tafsir Anwarul Bayan), trans. Afzal Hussain Elias and Muhammad Arshad Fakhri, (Karachi: Darul Ishaat, 2005), I, 434.

up for mankind. You command what is right and forbid what is wrong, and you believe in Allah." (3:110) By contrast, "the unbelievers among the people of the book," that is, the Jews and Christians who don't convert to Islam, "and the idolaters will remain in the fire of Gehenna. They are the most vile of created beings." (98:6).

The Muslims are the "best of people" insofar as they "command what is right and forbid what is wrong." The Jews (as well as the Christians and other unbelievers among the people of the book) are simply vile. What can follow from associating with them other than a share in the humiliation, poverty and disgrace that is their lot?

It is therefore with good reason, at least by the Qur'an's lights, that Allah warns the Muslims: "O you who believe, do not take as intimates anyone other than your own people, as they would spare no effort to ruin you, they love to interfere with you. Hatred is revealed by their mouths, but what their breasts hide is greater. We have made clear the signs for you, if you will understand." (3:118) Even worse, "You will find the Jews and the idolaters the most vehement of mankind in hostility to those who believe." (5:82) The Qur'an speaks of Jesus as a "messenger to the Children of Israel" (3:49), but instead of receiving him, the Jews only plot against him: "And they schemed, and Allah schemed, and Allah is the best of schemers." (3:54)

The Jews are so bold as to slander Islam: "Some of those who are Jews change words from their context and say, We hear and disobey, hear as one who does not hear, and Listen to us, distorting with their tongues and slandering religion. If they had said, We hear and we obey, hear and look at us, it would have been better for them, and more upright. But Allah has cursed them for their disbelief, so they do not believe, except for a few." (3:46)

They even dare to utter lies against Allah himself: "And indeed, there is a party of them who distort the book with their tongues, so that you might think that what they say is from the book, when it is not from the book. And they say, It is from Allah, when it is not from Allah, and they knowingly speak a lie about Allah." (3:78)

When Islamic societies falter, it is not the habit of the "best of people" to engage in introspection, at least beyond the proposition that they must redouble their efforts to please Allah. The idea of questioning their fundamental assumptions is rare in societies in which apostasy and heresy can bring imprisonment, serious injury, or even death. Allah tells the Muslims, "This day I have perfected your religion for you and completed my favor to you, and have chosen Islam as the religion for you." (5:3) Societies thus blessed with the perfect religion are unlikely to see that religion as the source of their troubles; they're much more likely to look to the teachings of that perfect religion for clues as to why they are not enjoying the prosperity that Allah promises to the faithful both in this world and the next.

And as far as many Muslim leaders are concerned, one chief answer to the question of why Islamic societies may not be enjoying the divine favor, aside from displeasing Allah with various sins, is because of the scheming of the Jews.

THE ESCHATOLOGICAL WAR AGAINST ISRAEL

These Qur'an passages are not obscure verses to which no one today pays attention. On August 23, 2024, at the Islamic Society of North Jersey in Flanders, New Jersey, an imam, Khalil Adem, declared, "You know, recently, all over YouTube influencers are talking about… They are starting to expose Israel for what it really is. All the secrets are starting to come out, some classified information even, and we are not going to get into that because that could fall under conspiracy theories, not worthy of a khutbah."[121]

Instead of talking about Israel, however, Adem turned to the depiction of the Jews in the Qur'an: "However, what we can say is that Allah told us about this the whole time in the Quran. He told us about the characteristics of the Jews. We didn't want to use 'Jewish' terminology—that word, 'Jewish'—because we are not hating anybody for their religion, but that was the way that Allah was labeling them at that time, and now we can narrow it down to Zionism, for example."[122]

That made it clear that he saw the Qur'an's writings as a key to understanding the contemporary geopolitical situation, particularly in reference to Israel. He said of the Jews: "We know the aggression that they have come with and we know their downfall. We know the verses [in the Quran] and Allah says they will be destroyed at the end. At the end their time will come, and the Muslims will be the ones to do it."[123]

Adem likely had in mind an Islamic tradition in which Muhammad is depicted as saying, "The last hour would not come unless the Muslims will fight against the Jews and the Muslims would kill them until the Jews would hide themselves behind a stone or a tree and a stone or a tree would say: Muslim, or the servant of Allah, there is a Jew behind me; come and kill him; but the tree Gharqad would not say, for it is the tree of the

121 "New Jersey Sermon By Khalil Adem: Allah Told Us About The Characteristics Of The Jews; He Said Their End Will Come—And Muslims Will Be The Ones To Do It; American Influencers Are Starting To Question Why Israel Controls Us While Muslims Are Labeled Terrorists," MEMRI, August 23, 2024, https://www.memri.org/tv/nj-friday-sermon-khalil-adem-youtube-influencers-ask-israel-controlling-america-jews-quran-end-come. Accessed October 30, 2024.

122 Ibid.

123 Ibid.

Jews."[124] The Jews must be killed because they are the ones who are standing between the Muslims and success, scheming against the Muslims and thwarting their plans. But Allah will give the Muslims victory in the end.

An imam in Canada, Adnan Abyat, preached a sermon in a similar vein in Coquitlam, British Columbia on August 2, 2024. First, he exhorted his audience to relieve the distress of the Muslim community by fighting for Islam: "I attest that Muhammad is Allah's servant and His prophet who awakened the desire for Jihad and incited the believers, who made Jihad for the sake of Allah the pinnacle of Islam, and the one who said that Paradise is underneath the shades of the swords. His shari'a elevated the status of the mujahideen and he said that Jihad for the sake of Allah raises a man a hundred levels in Paradise, and the distance between levels is like the distance between heaven and earth."

This led Abyat to think immediately of Hamas' war against Israel, and he added, "May Allah be pleased with the martyr, the persevering mujahid leader who lived as he wanted, free and proud—Ismail Haniyeh, may Allah have mercy on his soul."[125] He continued: "One of the highest qualities of a Muslim, one who believes in Allah and His Messenger, is to fight for the sake of Allah and to get killed as a martyr in the cause of Allah. There is

---

124 Imam Muslim, Sahih Muslim, trans. Abdul Hamid Siddiqi (New Delhi: Kitab Bhavan, revised edition 2000), 2922.

125 "Canadian Imam Adan Abyat: Jihad And Martyrdom Are The Pinnacle of Islam; Hamas Leader Haniyeh—A Mujahid And Martyr—Was Killed By The Jews, Who Killed Allah's Prophets And Tried To Kill Prophet Muhammad; May Allah Curse The Jews, Christian And Atheist Countries That Support Them; May Allah Annihilate Every Single Hypocrite Of The Islamic Nation," MEMRI, August 2, 2024, https://www.memri.org/tv/canadian-imam-adnan-abyat-jihad-pinnacle-islam-allah-curse-jews-martyr-ismail-haniyeh. Accessed October 30, 2024.

no life brighter than this life, and there is no death more honorable than this death; the death for [the sake of] Allah."[126]

The best target of this warfare would be the Jews, who are now fighting against Hamas in the same way that they fought against Muhammad. Abyat relates the fate of Hamas leader Ismail Haniyeh, who was killed in a highly secure guest house in Tehran, to that of the prophet of Islam:

> The one who is mocking him…You mock the Prophet. He was poisoned by the Jews…may Allah curse them. The same people who killed this brother, Ismail Haniyeh, may Allah have mercy on his soul, this leader, this chief, this mujahid—they tried to kill the Prophet before. So it is not new about them. The people who killed the prophets of Allah and the righteous people, and everyone who got killed by them, are showing us that they are only killing the mujahedeen for the sake of Allah, because they are frightened by them. They cannot face them so come and kill them by betraying them, using the hypocrites from our Islamic nation to guide them towards them. Without the hypocrites that we are living with, this could not achieve anything.[127]

Abyat concluded, "Oh Allah, act with cruelty against [the Palestinians] enemies—the Jews, plundering Zionists, Christians, and those who aid them. Oh Allah, annihilate the hypocrites of

---

126 Ibid.
127 Ibid.

the Islamic nation. Oh Allah, count them, kill them one by one, and do not leave a single one of them."[128] The failure of the Muslims to prevent the killing of Haniyeh did not lead Abyat or his comrades to consider that they were facing an extremely resourceful and indefatigable foe, and that they might not be wise to fight on. Instead, it only led Abyat to lionize Haniyeh in the most extravagant terms, by pointing out that he had been killed by the same evil people who had killed the prophet of Islam himself.

The portrayal of the Jews as the worst enemies of the Muslims in Islam's holy book also had the effect of situating Muslims' victories over Jews as eschatological victories, as signs of the divine favor. This idea also comes from the Qur'an, in which Allah claims credit for the victory of the Muslims over the pagan Quraysh in the Battle of Badr, the first great battle in Islamic history:

> When two parties of you almost fell away, and Allah was their protecting friend. In Allah let believers put their trust. Allah had already given you the victory at Badr, when you were contemptible. So observe your duty to Allah so that you may be thankful. When you said to the believers, Is it not sufficient for you that your Lord should support you with three thousand angels sent down? No, but if you persevere and avoid evil, and they attack you suddenly, your Lord will help you with five thousand angels sweeping in. Allah ordained this only as a message of good cheer for you, and that thereby

[128] Ibid.

> your hearts might be at rest. Victory comes only from Allah, the mighty, the wise. (3:122–6)

SACRED PLUNDER

In line with this, on March 8, 2024, the imam Fadi Yousef Kablawi, preaching at Masjid As Sunnah An Nabawiyyah in North Miami, Florida, painted a verbal picture of the Muslims enjoying the fruits of the Jews' labors as a sign of the victory that Allah had granted them over their foremost enemies. "Allah revealed to the messengers," Kablawi said, "instantly: 'We will defeat the oppressors, and We will make you the dwellers of their land, of their homes.'"[129]

Here Kablawi may have had in mind a Qur'an passage that describes Allah causing the people of the book to destroy their own homes and flee before the Muslims, who then enjoy what they abandoned as the spoils of war: "It is he who has caused those among the people of the book who disbelieved to go forth from their homes to the first exile. You did not think that they would go forth, while they thought that their strongholds would protect them from Allah. But Allah reached them from a place they did not expect, and cast terror in their hearts so that they ruined their houses with their own hands and the hands of the believers. So learn a lesson, O you who have eyes." (59:2) The Qur'an soon after refers to "What Allah gives as spoils to his messenger from the people of the towns." (59:7)

[129] "Friday Sermon By Florida Imam Dr. Fadi Kablawi: Oh Allah, Make This Ramadan A Blessed Month Of Victory; By Allah, We Will Seize, Enjoy, Live In The Jewish Settlements; We Will Inherit The Land, Homes, Property Of The Jews," MEMRI, March 8, 2024, https://www.memri.org/tv/floriday-imam-dr-fadi-yousef-kablawi-allah-make-blessed-ramadan-victory-seize-enjoy-live-jewish-settlements-inherit-land-home-property. Accessed October 30, 2024.

Kablawi related his statement about Allah giving the Muslims the homes of the Jews to the controversial "settlements" that Israelis were building on land that Palestinian Arabs were claiming for themselves, and issued a prediction: "By Allah, those settlements that they built, by Allah we will live in them.... By Allah, we will seize [them]. By Allah, we will enjoy [them]. By Allah we will live in [them]. If it is not us, our children will live in [them]. By Allah, the law of Allah and the *shari'a* of Allah will rule the land."[130] This he also related to the Qur'an: "And He caused you to inherit their land and their homes and their properties...' Yes. '...And have a land which you have not trodden.' [33:27] If it was land that the Muslims didn't seize before [in the time] of Banu Qurayza, then today it would be homes, buildings, and high-rises that we have never lived in."[131]

Kablawi thus sees the plundering of the Jews of today as a sacred act, one that helps bring the world more into line with the will of Allah. If the Muslims, or at very least the Palestinian Arabs, are (or claim to be) poor and dispossessed, the remedy is not to live somewhere in peace and begin producing something that will increase their wealth. The remedy is to focus hatred upon the Jews, and steal their possessions.

This is one reason why the modern state of Israel has had to maintain a war footing since the moment it was founded, and why its enemies are so implacable. In November 2011, one jihadist in Gaza put it in a prayer to Allah that was broadcast on Hamas' Al-Aqsa TV: "Praise be to you, our Lord. You have made our killing of the Jews an act of worship, through which we come

130 Ibid.
131 Ibid.

closer to you."[132] If fealty to Allah brings earthly prosperity and killing Jews is an act of fealty to Allah, then killing Jews brings earthly prosperity, not just in the form of their plundered property and land, but in further blessings from Allah for those who obey his commands.

132 "Islamic Militants in Gaza: Allah's Teachings Are the Fire with Which 'We Harvest the Skulls of the Jews'; 'We Move Closer to Allah through Blood, Body Parts, and Martyrs,'" MEMRI, November 3, 2011, https://www.memri.org/tv/islamic-militants-gaza-allahs-teachings-are-fire-which-we-harvest-skulls-jews-we-move-closer. Accessed October 30, 2024.

CHAPTER SEVEN

FAILURE BREEDS SUSPICION OF OUTSIDERS

BUYING FRIENDS

On December 26, 2004, a massive tsunami in South Asia killed 227,898 people, including 167,540 in Indonesia alone. US Secretary of State Colin Powell headed to one of the hardest-hit areas, the Indonesian city of Banda Aceh, on a mission to bring relief to those who were afflicted. On January 5, 2005, he sat down for an interview with Brian Williams of NBC Nightly News, and explained, "This is an area that will need a great deal of help. Food has to be brought in and we will arrange to bring in more food. We are pleased with the work that our helicopters are doing, and all of the Americans and other international relief agencies that are here and are doing such terrific work."[133]

133 Colin L. Powell, "Interview on NBC's Nightly News with Brian Williams," January 5, 2005, US Department of State Archive, https://2001-2009.state.gov/secretary/former/powell/remarks/2005/40343.htm. Accessed September 17, 2024.

Powell painted a picture of staggering American generosity: "President Bush has made it clear that we are going to do whatever it takes to help these countries get back up on their feet. The initial commitment was $350 million. This may require more."[134]

Williams, who was a far-left ideologue like all establishment media journalists, suggested that this generosity stood in contrast with the futile and wrongheaded war that the US was pursuing in Iraq at that time, largely at Powell's urging. Williams wondered if the compassion that the Americans were now demonstrating in Indonesia conflicted with the face that the nation was showing the world in Iraq: "Here are you, the American Secretary of State, sitting in a tent in the one nation in the world with the largest Muslim population. Those folks back in the States who were against the war in Iraq said, 'You know, we should have a different approach toward Muslims around the world, show a different face of the United States.' Is it a strange outgrowth of a disaster that people will see now this face of the United States?"[135]

Powell declined the opportunity to justify the US presence in Iraq, focusing instead on America's compassion: "Well, you know, the United States has always been a compassionate country. It is at the essence of our value system. So even if this wasn't a Muslim country or other Muslim countries involved in this tragedy, we would still be here to help, whether they were Christian or whatever."[136]

The secretary of state did acknowledge, however, that the disaster relief that the US was providing to Indonesia and the other countries that the tsunami devastated presented an opportunity: "But I think it will show to the Muslim world the nature

[134] Ibid.
[135] Ibid.
[136] Ibid.

of our society. But we've done a lot for the Muslim world. I mean, we rescued the Muslim people from the tyranny of the Taliban and al-Qaida in Afghanistan. We rescued them from the tyranny of Saddam Hussein. We rescued Muslims in Kosovo some years ago."[137]

Powell continued in this hopeful vein by expressing his high hopes for America's ill-fated democracy projects in Iraq and Afghanistan: "So I think if people will look at our actions and look at the subsequent results of those actions, and we see a democracy in Afghanistan and hopefully one in Iraq as well, people will judge us by what we end up accomplishing, and the anti-American feeling that we have seen in various parts of the world over the past year and a half will start to dissipate. I still think there is a reservoir of goodwill toward America and toward Americans. And certainly, when we have an opportunity to demonstrate how we can respond, that goodwill is reinforced."[138]

DON'T TRUST THEM

Powell would have done well to ponder a question and its answer that appeared on October 25, 2000, on AskImam.org, a popular website for Muslims to obtain guidance on their religion. The question (spelling and grammar as in the original):

> The west is often criticised by Muslims for many reasons, such as allowing women go to work.

137 Ibid.
138 Ibid.

> QUESTION
>
> But shouldnt the west also receive praise because its always them who intervenve when muslims r being tortured,they stopped Milosovic killing muslims and sent their own troops to the country,they r usually the first to send aid when theres a flood,they r also intervening in Isreal and condeming them killing Muslims ,so should we appreciate their efforts or not?[139]

The answer, which came from Mufti Ebrahim Desai of the site's "Fatwa Department," was succinct: "In simple the Kuffaar can never be trusted for any possible good they do. They have their own interest at heart."[140]

Colin Powell was almost certainly unaware of the fact, but the Qur'an states, "And the Jews will not be pleased with you, neither will the Christians, until you follow their religion. Say, Indeed, the guidance of Allah is guidance. And if you follow their desires after the knowledge that has come to you, then you would have from Allah no protecting guardian or helper." (2:120)

An imam in Detroit, Imran Salha, emphasized this in a Friday sermon on August 2, 2024. He began with a declaration of the preeminence of Islam: "Allah says: 'Certainly the disbelievers are distraught by the fact that your religion is superior.' Allahu

---

[139] "The west is often criticised by Muslims for many reasons, such as allowing women go to work," AskImam.org, October 25, 2000, https://askimam.org/public/question_detail/1394. Accessed on September 17, 2024.

[140] Ibid.

Akbar!"[141] Like other imams in the United States, as we saw in Chapter One, he held out Islam as the remedy for the nation's ills: "Islam is the last hope for America. Oh dear America.... Dear America, if you are looking for preservation, the way you treat Muslims around the world will dictate the longevity of your empire.... You cannot sustain morals without Islam, and Islam is the one true religion that will preserve morals."[142] It would do so, however, amid antagonism from adherents of rival religions: "The Christians and the Jews will never be fully accepting of you.... They may praise you. They may 'love' you between quotations. They may share causes with you. But these [that is, the Muslims] are your people.... You have two roles here in America: To Teach About Allah, and to frustrate the Zionists. Frustrate the Zionists with every single mode that is within your reach, as a citizen of this country.... They are the cockroaches of history, and we are the liberators."[143]

The Qur'an also tells Muslims, "Let not the believers take unbelievers for their friends in preference to believers. Whoever does that has no connection with Allah unless you are guarding yourselves against them, taking security. Allah bids you to beware of him. To Allah is the journeying." (3:28) Even more pointedly, it declares, "O you who believe, do not take the Jews and the Christians for friends. They are friends of one another. He among you who takes them for friends is of them. Indeed, Allah does not guide wrongdoing people." (5:51)

---

141 "Detroit Imam Imran Salha: Islam Is America's Last Hope; Muslims In The U.S. Have Two Jobs—Teaching About Allah And Frustrating The Zionists; They Are The Cockroaches Of History, And We Are The Liberators," MEMRI, August 2, 2024, https://www.memri.org/tv/detroit-imam-imran-salha-muslims-in-america-teach-allah-frustrate-zionists-cockroaches. Accessed October 30, 2024.

142 Ibid.

143 Ibid.

This reinforces the climate of suspicion that Imran Salha and so many other Islamic leaders have fostered. Faithful Muslims know to be wary of Jews and Christians, and to regard their friendly overtures with suspicion, for "Allah bids you to beware of them." A Muslim who takes the bait and becomes friends with them "is of them," that is, has become an unbeliever and has forfeited his place in paradise.

When non-Muslims such as Colin Powell came with hundreds of millions of dollars' worth of American aid, it was received, but with suspicion, not gratitude. This is because "And the Jews will not be pleased with you, neither will the Christians, until you follow their religion." At least some of the Muslims in Banda Aceh and elsewhere assumed, because of this Qur'anic passage, that Powell was bringing aid in order to entice Muslims away from Islam.

Even aside from the question of the overall intentions of infidels bearing gifts, Islam's intrinsic contempt for unbelievers creates a general sense of superiority that hampers genuine exchanges of ideas. What could "the best of people" possibly learn from "the most vile of created beings"?

In the Islamic mindset, a disaster such as the tsunami that hit South Asia in 2004 is a manifestation of the judgment of Allah upon a sinful people. If they had not sinned, they would have not suffered such a catastrophe, as the Qur'an says: "O you who believe, do not devour usury, doubling and quadrupling. Observe your duty to Allah, so that you may be successful." (3:130) Success thus comes from observing one's duty to Allah.

Powell had expressed the confidence that "people will judge us by what we end up accomplishing, and the anti-American feeling that we have seen in various parts of the world...will start to dissipate." If a Muslim who suffered through the tsunami, then became friendly with the unbelievers who were giving him humanitarian aid, he would only have been compounding the sin that brought on the tsunami in the first place.

Some Muslims even seize upon the giving of such aid as an opportunity to voice and encourage hatred of the givers. On March 7, 2024, Al-Jazeera Network featured an "influencer" named Gaza who called himself Abod, and who was enraged at the poor quality of the aid the Americans had given to the Gazans amid Hamas' war with Israel.

Abod began by reminding his followers that whatever appearances to the contrary there may be, America was not their friend: "Today, I will tell you about the Great Satan and the number-one enemy of our cause—America. America has supported Israel with a variety of equipment, and the most lethal weapons in the world. It supported Israel for free, so it can kill out Palestinian people. Can you imagine? Any resolution to force a ceasefire on Israel, is vetoed by them. It signals to Israel to shed Palestinian blood." He then belittled the aid the Americans had sent: "Ultimately, after five months have passed—we are entering the sixth—America felt pangs of conscience, so it sent some paltry aid, in a manner that is humiliating to people who were saved from a brutal attack. They dropped the aid from their airplanes in very small quantities. People, even Satan is shocked by what they did."[144]

This suspicion of the intentions of friendly outsiders, based on the Qur'an, has led to numerous attacks on medical personnel and those delivering food to the starving. On February 8, 2023, in Burkina Faso, Islamic jihadis opened fire on a Médecins Sans

[144] "Al-Jazeera TV Airs Video By Gaza Influencer 'Abod' Criticizing American Humanitarian Aid: The Aid Dropped By The 'Great Satan' And Our Number-One Enemy Was 'Paltry,' 'Humiliating,'" MEMRI, March 7, 2024, https://www.memri.org/tv/jazeera-qarar-american-aid-to-gaza-humiliating-palestinians-influencer-abod, Accessed October 30, 2024.

Frontières (Doctors Without Borders) medical team, killing two members of the team. Dr. Isabelle Defourny, the president of Médecins Sans Frontières, demonstrated that she had no understanding whatsoever of the Islamic mindset or the jihad ideology when she commented, "We are shocked and outraged by this killing. This was a deliberate and intentional attack on a clearly identified humanitarian team, during its medical work."[145] Yes, it was. But it was a humanitarian team made up of infidels; their assistance was not welcome.

A similar attack took place in September 2022, when the jihad group al-Shabaab carried out a carefully organized attack against a convoy of food trucks that were carrying supplies from the city of Baladweyne to the town of Mahas, murdering eighteen people.[146]

A polio worker was murdered in September 2024 in Pakistan when jihadis opened fire on a vaccination team.[147] In September 2022, four polio workers were murdered in Pakistan.[148] Eight polio workers were murdered in Afghanistan in February 2022.[149] In February 2013, a Muslim cleric was among those held for his

---

145 "2 aid group employees killed in Burkina Faso vehicle attack," Associated Press, February 8, 2023, https://apnews.com/article/politics-doctors-without-borders-burkina-faso-violence-fde421db6f93455aa1f08e470c574ba6. Accessed October 30, 2024.

146 "18 Killed in Bloody Al-Shabaab Attack," International Christian Concern, September 5, 2022, https://www.persecution.org/2022/09/05/18-killed-bloody-al-shabaab-attack/. Accessed October 30, 2024.

147 "Two killed in attack on Pakistani polio vaccination team," Reuters, September 11, 2024, https://www.reuters.com/world/asia-pacific/two-killed-attack-pakistani-polio-vaccination-team-2024-09-11/. Accessed October 30, 2024.

148 "Polio vaccination team attacked in Pakistan's Khyber Pakhtunwa; 4 dead," Times Now News, September 10, 2022, https://www.timesnownews.com/mirror-now/polio-vaccination-team-attacked-in-pakistans-khyber-pakhtunwa-4-dead-article-94116562. Accessed October 30, 2024.

149 "UN condemns brutal killing of eight polio workers in Afghanistan," UN News, February 24, 2022, https://news.un.org/en/story/2022/02/1112612. Accessed October 30, 2024.

involvement in the murder of at least nine women who were part of a polio vaccination team.[150]

In June 2012, a Pakistani Muslim cleric enunciated one reason why these attacks keep recurring. Maulvi Ibrahim Chisti termed the campaign against polio "un-Islamic" and called for jihad against the vaccination workers, saying jihad was the "only option," for the anti-polio campaign was a "Western conspiracy" to sterilize the Muslim population.[151] After the killing of yet another polio worker in Pakistan in March 2022, the Associated Press noted that "militants"—that is, Islamic jihadists—"often target polio teams and police assigned to protect them in Pakistan, falsely claiming the vaccination campaigns are a Western conspiracy to sterilize children."[152]

On September 17, 2024, the Taliban government in Afghanistan halted polio vaccination campaigns. The Taliban offered no reason for doing so, but the reason was nevertheless clear enough.[153]

Colin Powell had confidently predicted that "people will judge us by what we end up accomplishing, and the anti-American feeling that we have seen in various parts of the world…will start to dissipate." That did not turn out to be the case, and the reason why not was rooted in Islam.

---

150 Salisu Rabiu, "Nigerian reporters, cleric held after polio clinic killings," Associated Press, February 13, 2013, https://www.bostonglobe.com/news/world/2013/02/13/nigeria-journalists-charged-after-polio-killings/lbiWbITpgeuHGgDRpBM4QL/story.html. Accessed October 30, 2024.

151 "Pak cleric warns jihad against polio vaccination teams," Press Trust of India, June 13, 2012, https://www.rediff.com/news/report/pak-cleric-warns-jihad-against-polio-vaccination-teams/20120613.htm. Accessed October 30, 2024.

152 "Gunmen kill polio worker in Pakistan vaccination campaign," Associated Press, March 2, 2022, https://apnews.com/article/pakistan-gunmen-kill-police-polio-worker-northwest-7c027ca903c282ff3f0b82973cead3aa. Accessed October 30, 2024.

153 "Taliban suspends polio vaccination campaigns in Afghanistan, says United Nation [sic]," South Asia Terrorism Portal (SATP), September 17, 2024, https://www.satp.org/terrorism-update/taliban-suspends-polio-vaccination-campaigns-in-afghanistan-says-united-nation. Accessed October 30, 2024.

In 2014, a book was published in Malaysia that proved to be so enduringly popular that, seven years after its publication, it gained international attention for the open hostility to Christians that it fostered among Muslims. Distributed by the Selangor Islamic Religious Council (SIRC), which has links to the Malay government, *Pendedahan Agenda Kristian* (Exposing the Christian Agenda) declares that Christians were "enemies of Islam who are always malicious and display a negative attitude towards Muslims."[154] The Christians, the book states, "will try their best to cause heartache among Muslims."[155]

In line with Qur'an 2:120 and 5:51, the book states that "Christians will try their best to create resentment among the Muslims. Muslims must be stern and careful of Christians, and we must not follow or regard them as our protectors, leaders or guardians. If we are oblivious or doubtful of the truth about Islam, then it will be easier to be influenced by the lies of the Christians."[156]

In a video that was published online on January 6, 2020, Muhammed Korkmaz Hoca, an imam in Turkey, showed how such perspectives are instilled into Muslims from the earliest ages. "The other day," said Korkmaz, "somebody said to me: 'There are some good Jews.' [I said:] 'No, there are not.' He said: 'Yes, there are.' [I responded:] 'No, there aren't!' Why not? Because

154 Jules Gomes, "Malaysia: 'Christians Are Enemies of Islam,'" Church Militant, May 5, 2021, https://jihadwatch.org/2021/05/malaysia-government-agency-publishes-book-saying-christians-are-enemies-of-islam-who-are-always-malicious. Accessed October 30, 2024.

155 Ibid.

156 Ibid.

Allah himself said there aren't any. So how can I say that there are good [Jews]?"[157]

Korkmaz recounted how he trained his son to hate Jews:

> One day, I was waiting at the airport. We have a son, and he was five or six years old at the time.... Men with yarmulkes came.... They were fat. They sat across from us. Our son was running around, and they were laughing and making gestures like this. One of them took out 20 [Turkish lira] and gave it to our son. I said: "Son, come here. I'm going to tell you something. If you go over there, tear up that money, and throw it at their feet, then I will give you 50 lira...." He went over to them, tore up the money, threw it at their feet, and ran back to me. I showed them as I gave him 50 lira and I did this. I called my son. [I said:] "You see these dishonorable people? You know those children we see in Palestine who are killed, slaughtered, and raped?" [He said:] "Yes?" "These dishonorable people are the ones who kill them. Here they give you money to make themselves seem sympathetic, but if they have the opportunity, they will kill you, too. Beware! Do not love them."[158]

157 "Turkish Imam Muhammed Hoca: I Am Raising My Son to Be a High-Quality, Fantastic Enemy of the Jews and the Christians," MEMRI, January 6, 2020, https://www.memri.org/reports/turkish-imam-muhammed-hoca-i-am-raising-my-son-be-high-quality-fantastic-enemy-jews-and. Accessed October 30, 2024.

158 Ibid.

Warming to his topic, Korkmaz continued, "I am raising my son to be a very good, high-quality enemy of the Jews.... A fantastic enemy of the Jews, and a fantastic enemy of the Christians. 'A Muslim cannot raise an enemy.' Well, I am raising one, man! Is my brain not my own? I am their enemy. May the curse of Allah be upon them.... If I make my child love Jews and Christians, Allah will not say that I am good! Allah will not say this to me. Allah says: 'Do not incline toward them.' He says: 'Do not resemble them.' [The Quran says:] 'The Jews and the Christians will never approve of you until you follow their religion!'"[159]

He blamed Jews and Christians for the decline in morals: "Oh Muslims, did we not come into this condition because we resemble them? Our daughters have come to the point of walking in the streets completely naked. In the name of what? In the name of fashion.... They display their bodies in a way that does not please Allah or His Messenger. Was it not [the Jews] who propagated this? They did! And now am I going to have [my son] take 20 lira [from them]? Tear it up and throw it away! We do not need their money or their love. May Allah grant us hatred of them! We cannot love them. We love Muslims, for Allah says that only the believers are friends of one another. Allah says that only the believers are brothers of one another. Allah does not say that the Jews and Christians are our brothers. Why would I love them."[160]

Korkmaz assumed that in giving his congregation this advice, he was keeping them pure. But he was also cutting them off from ideas and associations that might have improved their earthly situation. As far as Korkmaz was concerned, the only way to do that was to serve Allah all the more ardently.

---

159 Ibid.

160 Ibid.

CHAPTER EIGHT

USING ISLAM TO MAKE A POINT

THE "FAR MORE SPLENDID" RELIGION

In the face of the catastrophic failure of Islam to create decent societies for its citizens, Westerners have long been ready with comforting fictions about the past (and present) glories of Islam. The tendency for non-Muslims in the West to explain away Islam's failures became more common after the defeat of Ottoman forces at the gates of Vienna on September 12, 1683, and the subsequent decline in Ottoman power, lessening the Islamic threat to Europe. Yet even while the Ottomans remained a very present threat to Europe, one prominent Christian European, Martin Luther, was ready to sing the praises of Islam.

In a 1550 preface to a book about Islamic religious practices, the great Reformer compared Islam favorably not just to the Roman Catholicism with which he was warring, but with Christianity and Christ himself:

> From this book, accordingly, we see that the religion of the Turks or Muhammad is far more splendid in ceremonies—and, I might almost say, in customs—than ours, even including that of the religious or all the clerics. The modesty and simplicity of their food, clothing, dwellings, and everything else, as well as the fasts, prayers, and common gatherings of the people that this book reveals are nowhere seen among us—or rather it is impossible for our people to be persuaded to them. Furthermore, which of our monks, be it a Carthusian (they who wish to appear the best) or a Benedictine, is not put to shame by the miraculous and wondrous abstinence and discipline among their religious? Our religious are mere shadows when compared to them, and our people clearly profane when compared to theirs. Not even true Christians, not Christ himself, not the apostles or prophets ever exhibited so great a display.
>
> This is the reason why many persons so easily depart from faith in Christ for Muhammadanism and adhere to it so tenaciously. I sincerely believe that no papist, monk, cleric, or their equal in faith would be able to remain in their faith if they should spend three days among the Turks. Here I mean those who seriously desire the faith

> of the pope and who are the best among them. The rest of the mob and the greater part of them, especially the Italians, those swine from the band of Epicurus, who believe absolutely nothing, are secure from every heresy and error, strong and invincible in their Epicurean faith, armed as much against Christ as against Muhammad or against even their own pope.[161]

Luther, however, was not really a sixteenth-century multiculturalist. He was quite critical of Islam in other contexts. In his 1528 treatise "On War Against the Turk," he wrote that "the people should be told of all the dissolute life and ways that the Turk practices, so that they may the better feel the need of prayer. To be sure, it has often disgusted me and still does, that neither our great lords nor our scholars have been at any pains to give us any certain knowledge about the life of the Turks in the two classes, spiritual and temporal; and yet he has come so near to us. For it is said that they too have chapters and monasteries. Some indeed have invented outrageous lies about the Turks in order to stir up us Germans against them, but there is no need for lies; the truth is all too great. I will tell my dear Christians a few things, so far as I know the real truth, so that they may the better be moved and stirred up to pray earnestly against the enemy of Christ our Lord."[162]

---

161 Sarah Henrich and James L. Boyce, "Martin Luther—Translations of Two Prefaces on Islam: Preface to the Libellus de ritu et moribus Turcorum (1530), and Preface to Bibliander's Edition of the Qur'an (1543)," Word & World, Vol. XVI, Number 2, Spring 1996, 259.

162 Martin Luther, "On war against the Turk," trans. anon, lutherdansk.dk. http://www.lutherdansk.dk/On%20war%20against%20Islamic%20reign%20of%20terror/On%20war%20against%20Islamic%20reign%20of%20terror1.htm. Accessed November 25, 2024.

Yet by 1550, Luther was professing admiration for Islam and using its alleged virtues as another weapon against papal loyalists and Roman Catholicism:

> So now be off with you, you tyrants and pontiffs, and for the sake of faith in Christ—i.e., for the sake of your ceremonies—kill, burn, suffocate, proscribe, and rage in full force, since here you see that the splendor of your ceremonies is no splendor at all alongside the excellent splendor of the Turks and that your customs are clearly an abomination when compared to theirs.
>
> Accordingly, it is likewise as a kind of apology for our gospel that we are publishing this book. For now I understand the reason why the Turkish religion is so concealed by the papists, why only base things are told of them. It is because they sense what in fact is true, that, if it should come to the point of arguing about religion, the whole papistry with all its trappings would fall. Nor would they be able to defend their own faith and at the same time refute the faith of Muhammad, since then they would have to refute those things that they themselves most approve and for which they most strive, and defend those things that the followers of Muhammad most approve and for which they most strive.[163]

[163] Henrich and Boyce, "Martin Luther," op. cit., 259–60.

Whatever Luther's motives in writing such things, he had become the founder not just of Protestantism, but of the Western practice of heaping praise upon Islam in order to denigrate something closer to hand. Many would follow in his footsteps.

THE "LESS IMPURE AND MORE REASONABLE" RELIGION

One was the renowned eighteenth-century French deist Voltaire, who disliked all religions but has become a favorite of modern-day Islamic apologists because he, like Luther, used Islam's alleged glories as a weapon in his denigration of Judaism and Christianity. In a 2008 article, a publication called *The American Muslim* boasted of the great rationalist's admiration for the religion of Muhammad:

> Voltaire plays a fascinating role as an early critic of all organised religions, a deist positing a God of reason, much like Islamic monism. His early tragedy Mahomet or Fanaticism portrays the Prophet as a Machiavellian manipulator but was really more a critique of the Catholic church and the use of religion to justify war. He later read Sale's newly translated Koran and came to an appreciation of Islam as "benign and tolerant," "a wise, severe, chaste and humane religion," "less impure and more reasonable" than Christianity and Judaism, having the eponymous Candide retire to an island near Constantinople to cultivate his garden and live in contemplation, much like a Muslim Sufi.

> Voltaire was even accused of being a "patriarch in the breast of Constantinople" for noting that the Ottoman empire "peacefully governs twenty peoples of different religions."[164]

The ex-Muslim scholar of Islam Ibn Warraq notes that Voltaire's English contemporary, the historian Edward Gibbon, likewise used Islam's greatness as a rhetorical weapon:

> Gibbon, like Voltaire, painted Islam in as favorable a light as possible to better contrast it with Christianity. The English historian emphasized Muhammad's humanity as a means of indirectly criticizing the Christian doctrine of the divinity of Christ. Gibbon's anticlericalism led him to underline Islam's supposed freedom from that accursed class, the priesthood. Indeed, the familiar pattern is reemerging—Islam is being used as a weapon against Christianity. Gibbon's deistic view of Islam as a rational, priest-free religion, with Muhammad as a wise and tolerant lawgiver, enormously influenced the way all Europeans perceived their sister religion for years to come. Indeed, it established myths that are still accepted totally uncritically by scholars and laymen alike. Both Voltaire and Gibbon

---

164 Eric Walberg, "Western Converts to Islam: Finding the inner Muslim prince," The American Muslim, April 2, 2008. http://theamericanmuslim.org/tam.php/features/articles/western_converts_to_islam_finding_the_inner_muslim_prince/0016060. Accessed November 25, 2024.

> subscribed to the myth of Muslim tolerance, which to them meant Turkish tolerance.[165]

Around the time that Voltaire and Gibbon were singing Islam's praises and marveling at its tolerance, a group of Coptic Christians set out on a pilgrimage to Jerusalem. To ensure their safety as they traveled, they requested and received a fatwa from the Grand Sheikh of al-Azhar, Egypt's venerable Islamic seminary, Abdallah al-Shabrawi, guaranteeing their safety and freedom to practice their religion. The Copts paid al-Shabrawi a thousand dinars for his generous gesture of tolerance.

Some other Muslims whom the Copts had not paid, however, were not so broadminded, and one of them told al-Shabrawi, "The deed you have authorized them to undertake will become a custom; next year they will make themselves a carpet and in future the Christians' pilgrimage will be spoken of in the same way as one talks of the Muslims' pilgrimage. Sheikh Abdallah, listen well to what I will tell you: you will carry the responsibility of this decision until the Day of the Resurrection."[166]

Alarmed, al-Shabrawi ignored his fatwa and told Muslims to attack the Copts. Students from al-Azhar joined in as a Muslim mob stoned and beat the Christian pilgrims and pillaged their camp. The pilgrimage was not completed, and the Copts did not dare to attempt such an endeavor in subsequent years.

Thus was the Islamic tolerance of which Luther, Voltaire and Gibbon sang.

Napoleon Bonaparte likewise professed love for Islam, but he intended not so much to denigrate other foes in the West by way

---

165 Ibn Warraq, Why I Am Not A Muslim (Amherst, New York: Prometheus Books, 1995), 21.

166 Ye'or, The Decline, op. cit., 380.

of comparing them to Islam, but instead to win over the people after his forces invaded Egypt in 1798. The invading French leader declared, "Glory to Allah! There is no other God but God; Mohammed is his prophet, and I am one of his friends.... The Koran delights my mind.... I love the prophet."[167] He claimed that a French-Egyptian alliance against the Mamluks was "the will of Mohammed."[168] Speaking to the Ottoman sultan, he accused the Russians of hating "those who believe in the unity of God, because, according to their lies, they believe that there are three," a reference to the Christian idea of the Trinity that Islam rejected.[169] Yet Napoleon did not convert to Islam. The whole thing was a political game, as he explained, "Fighting is a soldier's religion; I never changed that. The other is the affair of women and priests. As for me, I always adopt the religion of the country I am in."[170]

THE LEGENDARY MUHAMMAD OF SLEEPY HOLLOW

Those who propagated these myths wanted to use the fictionalized vision of a tolerant Islam as a weapon against a Western foe, by demonizing it in comparison, but this romanticized view of Islam took on a life of its own.

Aside from Napoleon's political calculations, Muhammad had for centuries been generally regarded in the West as an obvious false prophet, a self-serving manipulator who tailored the revelations he received to his own pecuniary and sensual advantage. In the nineteenth century, however, that began to change. The

167 Andrew Roberts, Napoleon: A Life (Westminster: Penguin Books, 2014), 201.
168 Ibid.
169 Ibid., 222.
170 Ibid., 199.

Scottish philosopher Thomas Carlyle decried the generally negative image that his contemporaries had of the prophet whom Islamic tradition depicts as sanctifying violence, marrying a child, taking sex slaves, and plundering the communities of those whom he regarded as his enemies. Carlyle waves all that away:

> Our current hypothesis about Mahomet, that he was a scheming Impostor, a Falsehood incarnate, that his religion is a mere mass of quackery and fatuity, begins really to be now untenable to any one. The lies, which well-meaning zeal has heaped round this man, are disgraceful to ourselves only. When Pococke inquired of Grotius, Where the proof was of that story of the pigeon, trained to pick peas from Mahomet's ear, and pass for an angel dictating to him? Grotius answered that there was no proof! It is really time to dismiss all that. The word this man spoke has been the life-guidance now of a hundred and eighty millions of men these twelve hundred years. These hundred and eighty millions were made by God as well as we. A greater number of God's creatures believe in Mahomet's word at this hour, than in any other word whatever. Are we to suppose that it was a miserable piece of spiritual legerdemain, this which so many creatures of the Almighty have lived by and died by? I, for my part, cannot form any such supposition. I will believe most things sooner than that. One would be entirely at a loss what to think of

> this world at all, if quackery so grew and were sanctioned here.[171]

Carlyle does not appear to realize the fundamental weakness of his argument: if the words Islam attributes to Muhammad were *not* "a miserable piece of spiritual legerdemain," then Christianity and other religions whom "so many creatures of the Almighty have lived by and died by" were themselves miserable pieces of spiritual legerdemain. The fact that millions or even billions of people believed something proved nothing of itself.

Carlyle wasn't alone in his admiration for Muhammad. The American storyteller Washington Irving, author of "The Legend of Sleepy Hollow" and "Rip Van Winkle," in 1850 published two books on Muhammad, *Life of Mahomet* and *Mahomet and His Successors*, in which he marvels that the prophet of Islam possessed "intellectual qualities" that were "undoubtedly of an extraordinary kind. He had a quick apprehension, a retentive memory, a vivid imagination, and an inventive genius."[172] Irving doesn't fail to mention some of the more scandalous elements of the Islamic traditions regarding Muhammad; he records, for example, both the Muslim prophet's marriage to the child Aisha and to his daughter-in-law Zainab. In describing these, Irving glosses over the scandalous aspects of both, and does his best to present Muhammad's behavior as above reproach.

In Aisha's case, Irving implies that she was sexually mature at age nine, when Muhammad consummated his marriage with her, and never considers whether the poor child had any opportunity to withhold her consent to be married to this man who was

---

171 Thomas Carlyle, "On Heroes, Hero Worship, and the Heroic In History," trans. Austin Meredith, 4, http://www.kouroo.info/kouroo/Carlyle/HEROES/8may40.pdf. Accessed November 25, 2024.

172 Washington Irving, Life of Mahomet (London: George Bell & Sons, 1874), 192.

forty-six years older than she. He also emphasizes Muhammad's love for her, as if that love was sufficient to overcome all the bizarre and revolting aspects of this episode:

> Ayesha, however, was but seven years of age, and, though females soon bloom and ripen in those eastern climes, she was yet too young to enter into the married state. He was merely betrothed to her, therefore, and postponed their nuptials for two years, during which time he caused her to be carefully instructed in the accomplishments proper to an Arabian maiden of distinguished rank.
>
> Upon this wife, thus chosen in the very blossom of her years, the prophet doted more passionately than upon any of those whom he subsequently married. All these had been previously experienced in wedlock; Ayesha, he said, was the only one who came a pure unspotted virgin to his arms.[173]

One would never get from this any idea of a man in his fifties using a child for his selfish sexual purposes. That aspect of the story is present, but so artfully hidden behind mists of romanticism as to escape notice altogether.

---

173 Ibid., 63.

CHAPTER NINE

TOLERANT ISLAM AS A SOCIAL AND GEOPOLITICAL WEAPON

THE MYTHICAL TOLERANT ISLAM

Historian Bat Ye'or identifies nineteenth-century geopolitical considerations as a chief impetus for the general propagation of the myth of a benign, expansive, tolerant Islam. She noted in 1995 a tendency that has only intensified since then: the coverup of the reality of Islamic history and theology in favor of a comforting myth. Bat Ye'or stated that "the long and agonizing process of Christian annihilation by the laws of jihad and dhimmitude—is a taboo history, not only in Islamic lands, but above all in the West. It has been buried beneath a myth, fabricated by Western politicians and religious leaders, in order to promote their own national strategic and economic interests."[174]

The fiction of Islam as a foundation for a multicultural and mutually respectful society "started in Bosnia-Herzegovina in the nineteenth century" in order to justify the French and British alliance with the Ottoman Empire against Russia during the Crimean War (1853–6), and has only grown since then. "We now have a myth which has taken the place of history, a big myth which has covered three continents: Africa, Asia, and Europe. This myth spans not only three continents but also 13 centuries, the period of Islamic rule over the Christian world."[175]

The British and French authorities believed that in order to sell their alliance with the Ottomans to their people, they had to construct a myth that would counter and destroy the general perception of the Turks as bloodthirsty, rapacious, and relentlessly imperialistic. The fiction that they constructed, according to Bat Ye'or, "alleges that Turkish rule over Christians in its European provinces was just and lawful. That the Ottoman regime, being Islamic, was naturally 'tolerant' and well disposed toward its Christian subjects; that its justice was fair, and that safety for life and goods was guaranteed to Christians by Islamic laws. Ottoman rule was brandished as the most suitable regime to rule Christians of the Balkans."[176]

---

174 Bat Ye'or, "Myths and Politics: Bosnia-Herzegovina and the Origin of the Myth of a Tolerant, Pluralistic Islamic Society," address to The International Strategic Studies Association, August 31, 1995, http://emperors-clothes.com/bosnia/bat.htm. Accessed December 2, 2024.

175 Bat Ye'or Interview by Michael Cromartie, "The Myth of Islamic Tolerance: Muslim 'protection' of Christians and Jews has actually been oppression, says scholar Bat Ye'or," Christianity Today, September-October 1998, https://www.christianitytoday.com/1998/09/myth-of-islamic-tolerance/. Accessed December 2, 2024.

176 Ye'or, "Myths and Politics," op. cit.

As the alternative to Turkish rule was Russian rule that the British and French considered to be against their interests, the Western Europeans painted a picture of the Turks as proto-multiculturalists. Bat Ye'or explains:

> To justify the maintenance of the Turkish yoke on the Slavs, it was portrayed as a model for a multi-ethnical and multi-religious empire. Of course, the reality was totally different! First the Ottoman Empire was created by centuries of jihad against Christian populations; consequently the rules of jihad, elaborated by Arab-Muslim theologians from the 8th to the 10th centuries, applied to the subjected Christian and Jewish populations of the Turkish Islamic dominions. Those regulations are integrated into the Islamic legislation concerning the non-Muslim vanquished peoples and consequently they present a certain homogeneity throughout the Arab and Turkish empires.[177]

Reality was exactly the opposite of this rosy picture: "although tolerance existed, it was counterbalanced by a system of oppression that led to the open extermination of Christian populations and the disappearance of the Eastern Christian culture. Tolerance was given to Jews and Christians only on the condition that they would accept and submit to a system of persecution and total inferiority. The governing context for such tolerance was the jihad. The two are linked and cannot be separated."[178]

---

[177] Ibid.

[178] "The Myth of Islamic Tolerance," Bat Ye'or Interview by Michael Cromartie, op. cit.

All that was ignored for another reason as well: the Western presence in Islamic lands. Bat Ye'or states, "The West's obfuscation was a result of the political and cultural difficulties of colonialism. France had North Africa, Algeria, Morocco, Tunisia, Syria, and Lebanon after World War I. England had a huge Islamic population in India and also in Egypt and Sudan, Iraq and Palestine. They didn't want to confront this population. They didn't want to protect the Christian minorities in these lands because they wanted to have an economically beneficial pro-Arab, pro-Islamic policy."[179]

As a result, the Europeans "didn't want to protect the Christians. They told them, You have to integrate into the Islamic environment; we are no longer protecting you. Therefore, for political, strategic, and economic reasons—mostly related to oil in the Middle East—the Western colonial powers didn't want to antagonize the Muslim countries. As a result, they developed a whole literature praising Islamic tolerance toward Jews and Christians."[180]

THE RELIGION OF "WONDERFUL VITALITY"

In Muslim countries, that literature was eagerly propagated. In January 1933, a journalist from an Ahmadi Muslim publication in Lahore, *The Light*, accosted the Irish playwright George Bernard Shaw aboard the luxury liner Empress of Britain and asked him to explain some remarks he had previously made about the

[179] Ibid.
[180] Ibid.

impending Islamization of Europe. "Stroking his silvery beard and looking at his watch," Shaw replied:

> I have always held the religion of Muhammad in high estimation because of its wonderful vitality. It is the only religion which appears to me to possess that assimilating capability to the changing phase of existence which can make itself appeal to every age. The world must doubtless attach high value to the predictions of great men like me. I have prophesied about the faith of Muhammad that it would be acceptable to the Europe of tomorrow as it is beginning to be acceptable to the Europe of today. The Medieval ecclesiastics either through ignorance or bigotry painted Muhammadanism in the darkest colours. They were in fact trained both to hate the man Muhammad and his religion. To them Muhammad was Anti-Christ. I have studied him—the wonderful man—and in my opinion far from being an Anti-Christ he must be called the Saviour of Humanity. I believe that if a man like him were to assume the dictatorship of the modern world he would succeed in solving its problems in a way that would bring it the much-needed peace and happiness.
>
> But to proceed: it was in the 19th century that honest thinkers like Carlyle, Goethe and Gibbon perceived intrinsic worth in the religion of Muhammad and thus there was some change

> for the better in the European attitude towards Islam. But the Europe of the present century is far advanced. It is beginning to be enamoured of the creed of Muhammad. In the next century it may go still further in recognising the utility of that creed in solving its problems and it is in this sense that you must understand my prediction. Already even at the present time many of my own people and of Europe as well have gone over to the faith of Muhammad, and the Islamization of Europe, to use the expression of your own query, may be said to have begun.[181]

Indeed it has. And the fact that Europe is largely so indifferent in the face of this world-historical phenomenon is due in great part to the view that Shaw and so many others like him in the West have presented regarding Islam. Nothing about jihad, dhimmitude, or Sharia. Nothing about the subjugation of women, the deeply rooted hatred of Jews, or the open-ended declaration of war against non-Muslim humanity. The West has been well instructed instead in the glories of Islam, and that instruction is having its desired effect.

JEWISH SCHOLARS' ROMANTICIZED ISLAM

As Western scholars began to study Islam in increasing numbers in the nineteenth century, Jewish scholars such as Ignaz Goldziher and Gustav Weil were among the pioneers of historical study of

181 "Bernard Shaw's Latest on Islam," The Light, vol. XII, nos. 4 and 5, January 24, 1933. https://www.ahmadiyya.org/islam/light-1933-jan-24-shaw.pdf. Accessed November 25, 2024.

the Islamic sources. Many Jewish scholars who undertook the study of Islam were also decidedly sympathetic to their subject.

The British politician Benjamin Disraeli, who was Jewish but was baptized in the Church of England at age twelve, was likewise a great admirer of Islam, and encouraged the new study of the religion in the West. The twentieth-century historian Bernard Lewis notes:

> One field in which the Jewish interest in Islam made a significant impact was that of scholarship. In the development of Islamic studies in European and, later, American universities, Jews, and in particular Jews of Orthodox background and education, play an altogether disproportionate role. In one of his early novels, Disraeli puts in his hero's mouth a lively plea for Oriental literatures: "Why not study the Oriental? Surely in the pages of the Persians and the Arabs we might discover new sources of emotion, new modes of expression, new trains of ideas, new principles of invention, and new bursts of fancy..." and praises "the Persians, whose very being is poetry, the Arabs, whose subtle mind could penetrate into the very secret shrine of nature." Jewish scholars did much to bring these achievements of the Islamic genius to Western notice, and inculcate in the Western mind a less prejudiced and more sympathetic understanding of Islam.[182]

[182] Bernard Lewis, "The Pro-Islamic Jews," Judaism: A Quarterly Journal of Jewish Life and Thought, vol. 17, no. 4, Fall Issue, 1968, 395.

Weil, says Lewis, published a biography of Muhammad in 1843, that differed from earlier European biographies in being "the first that was free from prejudice and polemic, based on a profound yet critical knowledge of the Arabic sources, and informed by a sympathetic understanding of Muslim belief and piety. For the first time, he gave the European reader an opportunity to see Muhammad as the Muslims saw him, and thus to achieve a fuller appreciation of his place in human history."[183] Lewis states of Jewish scholars of Islam that their role "in the development of every aspect of Islamic studies has been immense—not only in the advancement of scholarship, but also in the enrichment of the Western view of Oriental religion, literature and history, by the substitution of knowledge and understanding for prejudice and ignorance."[184]

Forsaking prejudice and achieving a more realistic view of Islam was all to the good, but Lewis also states that the Jewish scholars were known "sometimes to romanticize the merits and achievements of Muslim civilization in its great days."[185] The contemporary historian Martin Kramer says of the Jewish scholars that "in the aggregate, their approaches rested upon a heightened empathy and sympathy for Islam, conveyed to the rest of Europe through literature, exploration, and scholarship. And the common rationale, reduced to a sentence, was this: a Europe respectful of Islam and Muslims was more likely to show respect for Judaism and Jews."[186]

---

183 Ibid., 395–6.

184 Ibid., 397.

185 Martin Kramer, "Introduction," in The Jewish Discovery of Islam: Studies in Honor of Bernard Lewis, Martin Kramer, ed. (Tel Aviv: The Moshe Dayan Center for Middle Eastern and African Studies, 1999), pp. 1–48, https://martinkramer.org/reader/archives/the-jewish-discovery-of-islam/. Accessed December 2, 2024.

186 Ibid.

The goal was to make the case for the tolerance and equality of rights of Jews in Europe based on the glories, however exaggerated or mythical, of the Islamic world. If the Christians of Europe could appreciate Islamic wisdom and achievement, could they not accord the same respect to Jews and Judaism? "In myriad ways," Kramer notes, Jewish scholars "sought to emphasize Islam's splendor, as a strategy to remind Europe of the multiple origins of its own civilization, and its debt to Islam and Judaism. This meant a deliberate effort to associate Jews with those periods, places, and elements in Islamic civilization most admired by Europe. The message was straightforward: Jews had helped to bring the civilization of medieval Islam to its apex. Given the chance, they could do the same for the civilization of modern Europe. This interpretation of Islam, emphasizing its achievements and tolerance, had nothing in common with 'Orientalism' as ideology. Its purpose was to facilitate Europe's assimilation of Jews."[187]

Whatever its motive, the Jewish scholars' admiration for Islam was genuine and often quite profound. In Cairo in 1873, Goldziher had a profound religious experience in an Islamic context, writing in his diary: "In those weeks, I truly entered into the spirit of Islam to such an extent that ultimately I became inwardly convinced that I myself was a Muslim, and judiciously discovered that this was the only religion which, even in its doctrinal and official formulation, can satisfy philosophic minds."[188]

Goldziher studied at al-Azhar and says that those studies led him to adopt an Islamic perspective: "My formal way of thinking was through and through oriented toward Islam; subjectively,

[187] Ibid.

[188] John Tolan, "The Prophet Muhammad: A Model of Monotheistic Reform for Nineteenth-Century Ashkenaz," Common Knowledge 24:2, 2018, 271.

my emotional empathy also drew me hither. I called my monotheism Islam, and I did not lie when I said that I believed in the prophecies of Muhammad. My copy of the Qur'ān can bear witness to how I was inwardly inclined to Islam. My teachers earnestly awaited the moment of my open profession of faith."[189] Their anticipation was entirely reasonable, as Goldziher even prayed in a mosque alongside multitudes of Muslims and considered this a uniquely enriching experience: "In the midst of the thousands of the pious, I rubbed my forehead against the floor of the mosque. Never in my life was I more devout, more truly devout, than on that exalted Friday."[190]

Yet the great scholar did not convert to Islam. Instead, he sought to reform Judaism by bringing it in line with what he saw as the rationality of Islam: "My ideal was to elevate Judaism to a similar rational level. Islam, as my experience taught me, is the only religion, in which superstitious and heathen ingredients are not frowned upon by rationalism, but by orthodox doctrine."[191] Whatever he may have done for Judaism, Goldziher pioneered the scientific and historical study of the Hadith, paving the way for a thoroughgoing reevaluation of the historical reliability of the Islamic sources for Muhammad's life and words. His admiration of Islam never got in the way of his careful documentation of the historical value of the hadith accounts.

A twentieth-century European Jew who also admired Islam, Leopold Weiss, did go the whole way and convert. He recounted that while riding in "an upper-class compartment" on the Berlin subway in September 1926, he realized that wealth could not bring happiness:

---

189 Ibid., 272.
190 Kramer, "Introduction," op. cit.
191 Tolan, "The Prophet Muhammad," op. cit., 271.

> My eye fell casually on a well-dressed man opposite me, apparently a well-to-do businessman, with a beautiful briefcase on his knees and a large diamond ring on his hand. I thought idly how well the portly figure of this man fitted into the picture of prosperity which one encountered everywhere in Central Europe in those days: a prosperity the more prominent as it had come after years of inflation, when all economic life had been topsy-turvy and shabbiness of appearance the rule. Most of the people were now well dressed and well fed, and the man opposite me was therefore no exception. But when I looked at his face, I did not seem to be looking at a happy face. He appeared to be worried: and not merely worried but acutely unhappy, with eyes staring vacantly ahead and the corners of his mouth drawn in as if in pain—but not in bodily pain.[192]

Weiss scanned the other people in the compartment, "faces belonging without exception to well-dressed, well-fed people: and in almost every one of them I could discern an expression of hidden suffering, so hidden that the owner of the face seemed to be quite unaware of it."[193] When he got home, he recounts:

> I happened to glance at my desk on which lay open a copy of the Koran I had been reading earlier. Mechanically, I picked the book up to

[192] Leopold Weiss, The Road to Mecca (London: The Muslim Academic Trust, 1998), 308–9.

[193] Ibid., 309.

put it away, but just as I was about to close it, my eye fell on the open page before me, and I read:

> You are obsessed by greed for more and
> more
> Until you go down to your graves.
> Nay, but you will come to know! Nay,
> but you will come to know!
> Nay, if you but knew it with the knowl-
> edge of certainty,
> You would indeed see the hell you are
> in. In time, indeed, you
> shall see it with the eye of certainty:
> And on that Day you will
> be asked what you have done with the
> boon of life.

For a moment I was speechless. I think the book shook in my hands. Then I handed it to Elsa. 'Read this. Is it not an answer to what we saw in the subway?'

It was an answer: an answer so decisive that all doubt was suddenly at an end. I knew now, beyond any doubt, that it was a God-inspired book I was holding in my hand: for although it had been placed before man over thirteen centuries ago, it clearly anticipated something

> that could have become true only in this complicated, mechanized, phantom-ridden age of ours.[194]

Maybe, but Weiss could just as easily have found similar sentiments, stated more profoundly, in the scriptures of his own tradition, as well as in the Christian New Testament. Nevertheless, Leopold Weiss became Muhammad Asad, and produced a translation of the Qur'an, with accompanying commentary, that remains popular to this day; the Hamas-linked Council on American-Islamic Relations (CAIR) even distributes it to inquirers about Islam, despite (or perhaps because of) its massive bulk.

CAIR may also favor Asad's translation of the Qur'an because it is severely whitewashed, carefully smoothing over Islam's rough edges for Western non-Muslim readers. For example, the Qur'an states, "Indeed, those who believe, and those who are Jews, and Christians, and Sabeans, whoever believes in Allah and the last day and does right, surely their reward is with their Lord, and no fear will come upon them, neither will they grieve." (2:62)

The Qur'an seems to be particularly broad-minded here as it promises paradise to "those who are Jews or Christians or Sabeans." In his Qur'an, Muhammad Asad exults, "With a breadth of vision unparalleled in any other religious faith, the idea of 'salvation' is here made conditional upon three elements only: belief in God, belief in the Day of Judgment, and righteous action in life."[195] The requirement that an individual must become a Muslim to be saved is conspicuously lacking. Asad, however, subtly contradicts this idea when he renders this passage as guaranteeing paradise to

---

194 Ibid., 309–10.

195 Muhammad Asad, The Message of the Qur'an (Bristol, England, The Book Foundation, 2003), 21.

"those who have attained to faith in this divine writ," that is, the Qur'an itself.[196] This makes it clear that even Asad understands that the passage is not as generous as he himself attempted to lead his readers to believe. It actually assumes that the Jews, Christians, and Sabeans who enter paradise have become Muslims.

Asad's Qur'an also downplays or ignores altogether interpretations of the Islamic holy book that contradict his vision of a tolerant, pluralistic Islam. The Qur'an states: "Fight for the sake of Allah against those who fight against you, but do not transgress. Indeed, Allah does not love transgressors." (2:190) Asad claims that "this and the following verses lay down unequivocally that only self-defence (in the widest sense of the word) makes war permissible for Muslims."[197] He is silent about more traditional commentaries on the Qur'an such as the *Tafsir al-Jalalayn*, which asserts that this passage "was abrogated by *Surat at-Tawba*," that is, the Qur'an's sura 9, which features many reminders of the necessity of Muslims to wage armed jihad.[198] The *Tafsir al-Jalalayn* also reminds its readers of "Allah's words in the following *ayat*," that is, the following verse (2:191), which directs Muslims to "kill them wherever you find them."[199]

Weiss/Asad was not the first, and would not be the last, non-Muslim to convert to a fantasy Islam of his own making. Others who did not convert, meanwhile, shared in and expanded upon those fantasies.

---

196 Ibid.

197 Ibid., 51.

198 Jalalu'd-Din al-Mahalli and Jalalu'd-Din as-Suyuti, Tafsir al-Jalalayn, trans. Aisha Bewley (London: Dar Al Taqwa Ltd., 2007), 69.

199 Ibid.

CHAPTER TEN

THE AL-ANDALUS OF OUR DREAMS

THE MYTHICAL TOLERANT PAST

Particularly after the September 11, 2001, jihad attacks, a stream of books and articles began to appear that were designed to combat "Islamophobia" by enunciating soothing falsehoods about Islam. The secondary effect of this material, whether intentional or not, was to make Westerners ashamed of their own culture and heritage.

One of the most notorious examples of this is the myth of tolerant, pluralistic al-Andalus—medieval Muslim Spain. Historian, scholar of religions, and Islamic apologist Karen Armstrong has claimed that "until 1492, Jews and Christians lived peaceably and productively together in Muslim Spain—a coexistence that was impossible elsewhere in Europe."[200] One key originator of this persistent myth was the historian María Rosa Menocal, whose 2002 book *The Ornament of the World: How Muslims, Jews, and Christians Created a Culture of Tolerance in Medieval Spain* became a widely cited and much beloved reinforcement for the post-9/11 West's fantasies that a mutually beneficial accommodation could be found with the Islamic world.

Yossi Klein Halevi, author of the relentlessly hopeful *At the Entrance to the Garden of Eden: A Jew's Search for God with Christians and Muslims in the Holy Land*, was enthusiastic about *The Ornament of the World*, saying it was "essential reading" for "all those who believe that religion still has a role to play in helping humanity heal and evolve."[201] The renowned educator Harold Bloom wrote the Foreword to *The Ornament of the World*, expressing sorrow over the fact that "there are no Muslim Andalusians visible anywhere in the world today."[202]

Indeed. But were there ever any? Menocal's book is more myth and wishful thinking than fact, and that appears to be at least partly intentional; she even begins *The Ornament of the World* with the hoary opener of all fairy tales, "Once upon a time...."[203] She asserts that Andalusia remains a source of "our cultural memories and possibilities,"[204] but what she offers is actually more possibility than memory. Menocal claims that the Muslim overlords of al-Andalus "not only allowed Jews and Christians to

200 Karen Armstrong, "The curse of the infidel: A century ago Muslim intellectuals admired the west. Why did we lose their goodwill?" Guardian, June 20, 2002, https://www.irfi.org/articles/articles_301_350/curse_of_the_infidel.htm. Accessed October 30, 2024.

201 Yossi Klein Halevi, book jacket of María Rosa Menocal, The Ornament of the World: How Muslims, Jews, and Christians Created a Culture of Tolerance in Medieval Spain (Boston: Little, Brown), 2002.

202 Harold Bloom, "Foreword," in Menocal, op. cit., 15.

203 Ibid., 5.

204 Ibid., 281.

survive but, following Quranic mandate, by and large protected them.... In principle, all Islamic polities were (and are) required by Quranic injunction not to harm the dhimmi, to tolerate the Christians and Jews living in their midst."[205]

Yet she undercuts this when she describes exactly what it meant to be a dhimmi:

> The *dhimmi*, as these covenanted peoples were called, were granted religious freedom, not forced to convert to Islam. They could continue to be Jews and Christians, and, as it turned out, they could share in much of Muslim social and economic life. In return for this freedom of religious conscience the Peoples of the Book (pagans had no such privilege) were required to pay a special tax—no Muslims paid taxes—and to observe a number of restrictive regulations: Christians and Jews were prohibited from attempting to proselytize Muslims, from building new places of worship, from displaying crosses or ringing bells. In sum, they were forbidden most public displays of their religious rituals.[206]

Reality was even worse than this. Historian Kenneth Baxter Wolf notes that the restrictions on the dhimmis were designed to establish and protect "the dominant position of Islam."[207] In line with this imperative, "aside from such cultic restrictions most of the laws were simply designed to underscore the position of

205 Ibid., 29–30.

206 Ibid., 72–3.

207 Kenneth Baxter Wolf, Christian Martyrs in Muslim Spain (Cambridge: Cambridge University Press, 1988), 12.

the dimmîs as second-class citizens."[208] Wolf points out that Paul Alvarus, a Christian who lived under Muslim rule in Córdoba in the ninth century, complained bitterly about the "unbearable tax" that he was as a Christian required to pay to the Muslim rulers.[209] Wolf also quotes another Christian complaining about the tax, and states, "there is little doubt, given the tone of victimization that both men adopted when speaking of the levies and the regularity with which they were collected, that *tributum, vectigal,* and *census* were simply Latin synonyms for the universal *dhimmî* tax, the *jizya.*"[210]

The reality of al-Andalus was precisely the opposite of Menocal's fairy tales. Historian Richard Fletcher states that "the simple and verifiable historical truth is that Moorish Spain was more often a land of turmoil than it was a land of tranquility." Contrary to what Westerners of the twenty-first century so desperately wanted to believe, "Moorish Spain was not a tolerant and enlightened society even in its most cultivated epoch. The Mozarabic Christian communities whom John of Gorze met on his embassy to Córdoba were cowed and demoralized.... The Christians of al-Andalus were second-class citizens like Christians under Muslim rule elsewhere in the world such as the Copts of Egypt."[211]

As in our own day, the rulers of Muslim Spain were zealous to punish criticism of Islam and its prophet. Even Menocal concedes that they had "zero tolerance for disparagement of their Prophet."[212] Wolf provides an example: "In the spring of 850, a priest named Perfectus was arrested and later executed for publicly

---

208 Ibid., 9, 10.
209 Ibid., 12.
210 Ibid.
211 Richard Fletcher, Moorish Spain (Berkeley: University of California Press, 1992), 172–3.
212 Menocal, op. cit., 70.

expressing his opinions about the errors of Islam to a group of Muslims. Months later a Christian merchant named Joannes suffered a severe lashing, public humiliation, and a long prison term for invoking the prophet's name as he sold his wares in the marketplace."[213] After this, the Muslims embarked upon an orgy of executions of Christians who had been accused, rightly or wrongly, of blasphemy; nevertheless, Menocal finds a way to look on the bright side, noting that after about fifty of these executions, "the passions of the moment passed and life went on as it had before in this city of thriving religious coexistence."[214]

Not always. If the dhimmis forgot their place, the punishment could be swift and severe. In 1066, the Muslim king of Granada, Badis ibn Habus, appointed a Jew, Samuel ibn Naghrillah, his vizier. The Muslims of Granada were incensed, for a non-Muslim to hold authority over Muslims was a violation of Islamic law. A Muslim jurust, Abu Ishaq, was outraged at this clear violation of Islamic law to the extent that he was moved to compose a poem that stands today as model of the Islamic tolerance that Western politicians are so fond of invoking:

> He has chosen an infidel as his secretary when he could, had he wished, have chosen a Believer. Through him, the Jews have become great and proud and arrogant—they, who were among the most abject. And have gained their desires and attained the utmost and this happened suddenly, before they even realized it. And how many a worthy Muslim humbly obeys the vilest ape among these miscreants. And this

213 Wolf, op. cit., 12.
214 Menocal, op. cit., 70.

did not happen through their own efforts but through one of our own people who rose as their accomplice. Oh why did he not deal with them, following the example set by worthy and pious leaders?

Put them back where they belong and reduce them to the lowest of the low, Roaming among us, with their little bags, with contempt, degradation and scorn as their lot, Scrabbling in the dunghills for colored rags to shroud their dead for burial...These low-born people would not be seated in society or paraded along with the intimates of the ruler....God has vouchsafed in His revelations a warning against the society of the wicked. Do not choose a servant from among them but leave them to the curse of the accursed! For the earth cries out against their wickedness and is about to heave and swallow all.

Turn your eyes to other countries and you will find the Jews are outcast dogs. Why should you alone be different and bring them near when in all the land they are kept afar?... I came to live in Granada and I saw them frolicking there. They divided up the city and the provinces with one of their accursed men everywhere. They collect all the revenues, they munch and they crunch. They dress in the finest clothes while you wear the meanest. They are the trustees of your secrets, yet how can traitors be trusted?

> Others eat a dirham's worth, afar, while they are near and dine well....
>
> Their chief ape has marbled his house and led the finest spring water to it. Our affairs are now in his hands and we stand at his door. He laughs at God and our religion....
>
> Hasten to slaughter him as an offering, sacrifice him, for he is a precious thing....Do not consider it a breach of faith to kill them, the breach of faith would be to let them carry on. They have violated our covenant with them....God watches His own people and the people of God will prevail.[215]

Enflamed by Abu Ishaq's verses, Muslim mobs rampaged through Granada, hunting for Jews, ultimately murdering around four thousand, but even this did not shake Maria Rosa Menocal from her determination to see al-Andalus as a paradise of tolerance; she waved away the Granada pogrom as a "relatively isolated Muslim uprising against what had been a warmly favored Jewish community."[216]

The mobs were acting in accord with provisions of Sharia that remain in force to this day. A Saudi jurist, Manaa K. al-Qubtan, issued a fatwa in 1993 in which he declared, "The command of a non-Muslim over a Muslim is not permitted based on the words

215 Darío Fernández-Morera, The Myth of the Andalusian Paradise, (Wilmington, Delaware: ISI Books, 2016), 182–83.

216 Menocal, op. cit., 135.

of Allah: 'and Allah will not open to the unbelievers against the believers a way.' [Sura 4:140]"[217]

Nevertheless, the myth of a tolerant al-Andalus could not be sidetracked. It entered the mainstream, even gaining the endorsement of the president of the United States. Speaking in Cairo on June 4, 2009, Barack Obama declared, "Islam has a proud tradition of tolerance. We see it in the history of Andalusia."[218]

Yet one massive problem with this persistent and widespread fantasy is that it leads only to embarrassing questions. If Obama was correct that Islam had a proud tradition of tolerance, why were Islamic societies so notoriously intolerant in our own age? If al-Andalus was really a demonstration of the true and benign face of Islam: a paradise of proto-multiculturalism in which Jews, Christians, and Muslims all celebrated diversity together, appreciating one another's variegated gifts, why was Muslim Spain singular in Islamic history? Why hasn't anyone come up with another example of a tolerant, pluralistic Islamic society?

STEALING FROM THE MUSLIMS

The myth would expand and combine with other myths. Not only was al-Andalusia tolerant at a time when Christian Europe was supposedly much less so, even worse, the Western world shamelessly stole whatever it managed to accomplish from the Islamic world. In August 2020, the UK's *Guardian* provided a striking example of this additional fantasy in a lengthy, breathlessly

[217] Mannaa K. al-Qubtan, "Saudi Arabia: Fatwa for non-Muslims," in Bat Ye'or, Islam and Dhimmitude, Miriam Kochan and David Littman, trans. (Madison, New Jersey: Fairleigh Dickinson University Press, 2002), 411.

[218] Barack Obama, "Remarks by the President on a New Beginning," Cairo, June 4, 2009, https://obamawhitehouse.archives.gov/the-press-office/remarks-president-cairo-university-6-04-09. Accessed September 19, 2024.

enthusiastic article entitled, "Looted landmarks: how Notre-Dame, Big Ben and St Mark's were stolen from the east."[219] It stated that those architectural masterpieces were "beacons of western civilisation. But, says an explosive new book, the designs of Europe's greatest buildings were plundered from the Islamic world—twin towers, rose windows, vaulted ceilings and all."[220]

It was ironic that the *Guardian* was lamenting the alleged fact that the West had plundered these treasures from the Islamic world, when there were actually Muslim preachers calling upon Muslims to plunder Jews, but on that the *Guardian* was silent.

The *Guardian* article highlights the "discoveries" of a "Middle East expert" named Diana Darke, author of a book called *Stealing from the Saracens*, which the *Guardian*'s Oliver Wainwright called "an exhilarating, meticulously researched book that sheds light on centuries of borrowing."[221]

"Borrowing" is a more polite word than Diana Darke herself used, but otherwise Wainwright is completely on board with her project, reporting her dismay at finding that it was not common knowledge in the West that everything we have, everything we have done, everything we have made, has come from Islam: "I was astonished at the reaction," she lamented. "I thought more people knew, but there seems to be this great gulf of ignorance about the history of cultural appropriation. Against a backdrop

219 Oliver Wainwright, "Looted landmarks: how Notre-Dame, Big Ben and St Mark's were stolen from the east," Guardian, August 13, 2020, https://www.theguardian.com/artanddesign/2020/aug/13/looted-landmarks-notre-dame-big-ben-st-marks-east-stealing-from-the-saracens?utm_term=9582d30cdefb65bf1df7ffc8a7ab6b9c&utm_campaign=GuardianTodayUK&utm_source=esp&utm_medium=Email&CMP=GTUK_email. Accessed October 30, 2024.

220 Ibid.

221 Ibid.

of rising Islamophobia, I thought it was about time someone straightened out the narrative."[222]

Of course. And who better to do such a thing than Diana Darke, a favored popular intellectual who was frequently featured on the BBC, as well as in the *Guardian*? It was easy to see why she would be the British intelligentsia's favorite "Middle East expert": her book's ridiculous claims are yet more examples of the British elite's ongoing efforts to compel Britons to believe that Islam was part of their own culture and heritage, so that they would be shamed into accepting without protest mass Muslim migration into Britain, as well as jihad violence and Sharia oppression of women. It was just more of Britain's continuing cultural suicide.

In this case, the deception and sleight of hand were clumsy and obvious. The subtitle of the *Guardian* article claimed that "the designs of Europe's greatest buildings were plundered from the Islamic world." A centerpiece of Diana Darke's case for that was that "Notre-Dame's architectural design, like all gothic cathedrals in Europe, comes directly from Syria's Qalb Lozeh fifth-century church."[223]

A fifth-century church. Islam arose in the seventh and eighth centuries. What exactly did the design of a pre-Islamic church in Syria have to do with the Islamic world? Nothing whatsoever. It just happens that the site of this church was conquered by Muslims several centuries after it was built, so for Diana Darke, the *Guardian*, and their luckless readers, this became an example of how the West "stole from" or "plundered" the Islamic world.

[222] Ibid.
[223] Ibid.

Even more ridiculous was the claim that the Dome of the Rock in Jerusalem was the basis for church architecture in Europe, when the Dome of the Rock itself was patterned after the great cathedral in Constantinople, Hagia Sophia. St. Mark's in Venice was also patterned after Hagia Sophia, although Darke claimed it was based on the Dome of the Rock. The interior of St. Mark's is covered on virtually every available space with Christian art, as was the interior of Hagia Sophia. Which is its more likely influence? If those who built St. Mark's were imitating the Dome of the Rock, why didn't they opt for a more austere interior?

In November 2024, a politely skeptical reviewer, Mathew Lyons, asked in the *Telegraph*, "But is it true that Romanesque architecture's debt to Muslim craftsmen is so great that we should rename the style Islamesque, as Diane Darke argues in her book of the same name?"[224] Lyons notes that "one problem with Darke's thesis, however, is that many of these were also found in Byzantium, the eastern half of the former Roman empire, which was still a major power at the turn of the millennium."[225] Darke argues that by the time of the construction of the marvels of Western architecture that she thinks betray Islamic influence, Western Europe had largely forgotten about Byzantium and was embroiled in conflicts with the Ottoman Turks.

The second half of her claim is undoubtedly true, but the first is completely false. The Council of Florence in the 1440s sparked the Renaissance, as the neo-Platonist philosopher Gemistos Plethon traveled with the Orthodox delegation from Constantinople to Italy. Once there, Gemistos, who was not a theologian and was

---

224 Mathew Lyons, "Should we thank Islam for the most beautiful buildings in Christendom?," Telegraph, November 25, 2024, https://www.yahoo.com/lifestyle/thank-islam-most-beautiful-buildings-131500724.html. Accessed November 25, 2024.

225 Ibid.

bored with the proceedings of the council, began to give lectures on Plato to rapt audiences in Florence. The Byzantine Roman influence was stronger than ever in Western Europe at precisely the time that Diana Darke, apparently unaware of all this, was pronouncing it dead. Lyons writes, "In Sicily, she downplays the existence of a large community of Byzantine Greeks, present on the island since the sixth century, under both Islamic and Norman dominion. 'In no other European location ..was there such a thorough mingling of Arab and Norman peoples and cultures,' she writes, as if the Byzantines weren't there at all."[226]

For her, they weren't.

CULTURAL SELF-ABNEGATION

The nonsense from Diana Darke was part of a much larger effort. Another example of the same cultural self-abnegation came in October 2019, when the British Museum unveiled a lavish exhibition called "Inspired by the East," about how Western art had been massively influenced by Islamic art. "Charting the fascinating history of cultural and artistic interactions between East and West," the Museum explained, "this exhibition explored the impact of the Islamic world on Western art for centuries."[227]

The Museum explained that "artistic exchange between East and West has a long and intertwined history, and the exhibition picked these stories up from the fifteenth century, following cultural interactions that can still be felt today."[228]

226 Ibid.

227 "Inspired by the east: how the Islamic world influenced western art," British Museum, https://www.britishmuseum.org/exhibitions/inspired-east-how-islamic-world-influenced-western-art. Accessed September 18, 2024.

228 Ibid.

Never mind that the Islamic influence on Western art was severely limited by the fact that Sharia forbids representation of living creatures. That fact might have reflected negatively upon Islam and Sharia, and was left unstated.

Did the British Museum host an exhibition on how Western art influenced the Islamic world, a topic about which there is a great deal that could be said, ranging from the cultural appropriation of Byzantine church architecture to the stylistic similarities of Shi'ite iconography to Western art? Of course not. The objective was to get Westerners to despise their own heritage, not revere it.

The British Museum, Diana Darke and the *Guardian* did the British public, and people all over the Western world, a grave disservice by misleading them about their own culture and heritage, and doing so in a way that is designed to render them complacent and defenseless in the face of a genuine threat of jihad violence and Sharia oppression.

But the problem went far beyond the museum, the newspaper, and the writer.

CHAPTER ELEVEN

THEY INVENTED SCIENCE, YOU KNOW

THE ADVANCED UMMA, THE BENIGHTED WEST

The British Museum exhibit and the *Guardian* article were just two manifestations of the larger trend in the West today of non-Muslims dissembling about history in order to cover for the failure of Islam.

Many of those who present these falsehoods don't even seem to be aware of how false they really are. That was the case with the TikTok star GeoHussar, who had 260,000 followers as of September 2024, and who bills himself as "NATO summit 2024 Invitee and Attendee.... Dispeller of Fearmongers."[229] He also says, "I'm just a regular dude whose [sic] been reading world history and current events pertty [sic] hardcore for the past few decades. I have a degree in econ and another one in mathematics.

[229] GeoHussar, YouTube channel, https://www.youtube.com/@GeoHussar. Accessed September 21, 2024.

I got my MS in Analytics and use those skills to observe and discuss whats [sic] going on in the world. Most of the time, I use these skills to dispel [sic] the ocean of fear that the media and many influencers generate."[230]

As a reliable weathervane of cultural trends, his video warrants a brief examination. This TikToker's ignorance of basic facts of history, and his false assumptions about so much of it, are more or less typical of the low state of education in the twenty-first century. Multitudes of his generation have been taught all the nonsense he peddles in this video as if it were fact; they've likewise been told that non-Western, non-Christian civilizations, particularly Islamic civilization, were vastly superior.

On July 2, 2024, GeoHussar published a video entitled "Which #religion brought more to western civilization #Christianity or #Islam?"[231] He answers this question in the first seconds of his video, and proceeds to demonize the Roman Catholic Church for its supposedly anti-science stance: "Which religion advanced Western Civilization more: Christianity or Islam? The answer is Islam and it's not even a question. You might be thinking that Europe made all of these advancements and they were Christian nations, and it's true: Europe was Christian and they made all of these scientific advancements, but they did that in spite of the Church. Galileo, Dante, Marco Polo, Giordano Bruno were all great thinkers, scientists and mathematicians who were imprisoned or executed by the Church because their teachings went against dogma."[232]

230 GeoHussar, Patreon, https://www.patreon.com/geohussar/about?l=es. Accessed September 21, 2024.

231 GeoHussar, "Which #religion brought more to western civilization #Christianity or #Islam?," YouTube channel, July 2, 2024, https://www.youtube.com/watch?v=Rtg-s896P9EQ. Accessed September 21, 2024.

232 Ibid.

This is wildly overstated. There is no evidence that the Church imprisoned or executed Dante or Marco Polo. Marco Polo was indeed imprisoned, but not for heresy; while fighting for Venice in its war against Genoa, he was captured and held as a prisoner of war. Bruno was indeed executed for heresy, but this was because of his views on Catholic beliefs such as the divinity of Christ and transubstantiation, not his scientific explorations.

Even Galileo's case is not quite as cut and dried as the TikTok star told his followers. Some of Galileo's most fervent supporters were astronomers who were not secular—they were Jesuits. Cardinal Maffeo Barberini, who later became Pope Urban VIII, the very pope who clashed with Galileo, was an early supporter of his work to establish the truth of the idea that the earth revolved around the sun, and not the other way around. Historian Jerome Langford observes that Urban VIII and other Roman Catholic hierarchs "believed that Galileo might be right, but they had to wait for more proof."[233]

A bit later in his video, GeoHussar says, "Now let's go back to the Middle Ages, between 500 to let's say 1300, when all of Europe was united by the same kind of Christianity. The countries were still warring brutally with one another. Most of the population was illiterate, and any teachings and breakthrough that remotely contradicted what the clergy was saying was shut down in Christian Europe. The Bible was written in Latin, which only a small percentage of the population was able to understand, so if you were a regular farmer, you would just have to trust the priest to say, 'Yes, what I'm reading to you is actually in the Bible,'

233 Thomas Woods, How the Catholic Church Built Western Civilization (Washington, DC: Regnery, 2005), 71.

while in the caliphates, the Qur'an was written in Arabic, and if you could read Arabic, you could read the word of God."[234]

This is a variation on the all-too-common theme of benighted Westerners versus noble and intelligent non-Westerners, and it's just as vacuous in this context as it is when used in connection with the native inhabitants of North and South America. It is unclear whether this TikTok star is aware that the Bible was originally translated into Latin in the fourth century in order to render it more, not less, accessible to the common people, who spoke that language at the time. As Latin gradually developed into Spanish, French, Italian, Romanian and the smaller Romance languages, Latin continued to be the liturgical language of the Roman Catholic Church, not in order to conceal the Church's teachings, but to preserve its unity and guard against heresies developing from simple mistranslation.

GeoHussar also betrays Protestant assumptions when he suggests that priests would mislead their people as to what the Bible said, when neither the Roman Catholic Church nor the Orthodox Church ever held to the Protestant doctrine of *sola scriptura*, and so they would not have felt any need to make any such claim until the time of the Protestant Reformation, which began over two hundred years after the period GeoHussar is addressing.

In line with all this, although he happily notes that in the caliphates, the Qur'an was written in Arabic, and "if you could read Arabic, you could read the word of God," but doesn't appear to be aware of the fact that in the Islamic caliphates of the past—as well as in many Muslim countries today—the vast majority of the inhabitants are not Arabs, and do not speak Arabic as a native

[234] GeoHussar, "Which #religion," op. cit.

language. The five countries today with the largest Muslim populations are Indonesia, Pakistan, India, Bangladesh and Nigeria; none of them are Arab countries. When young boys in those countries begin to memorize and recite the Qur'an, they are often mouthing syllables without having any idea what exactly they're reciting.

This was no less true in the Abbasid caliphate (750–1258), which was comprised at its height of the territories comprising the present-day nations of Iran, Pakistan, and other notably non-Arab polities. The people there were no less cut off from a direct experience of the Qur'an than a medieval Christian who did not speak Latin was from the Vulgate.

Unaware of all this, GeoHussar digs in deeper: "While the Christianization of Europe just led to more war and barbarity, unity was actually taking place in the Middle East and Northern Africa. The ancient cultures of Persia and Egypt merged with the center at Baghdad…the largest and most prosperous, cultured city in the world."[235] Baghdad, he claimed, was a center of learning unrivalled anywhere in Europe: "For centuries under the Abbasid caliphate, the three cities during the Middle Ages with the best universities in the world were Baghdad, Cairo and Córdoba. Those universities existed two centuries before the first one in Europe, which was either Oxford or the one at Bologna. No city on Earth today could compare to what Baghdad was. It would have been a combination of New York, Tokyo and the Vatican."[236]

This is a common claim: that while the West is ascendant today, this wasn't always the case, and there was a time when

[235] Ibid.
[236] Ibid.

Europeans were blowing their noses into their hands while non-Europeans were exploring the finer points of astronomy and philosophy. The agenda of such claims is clear: they're designed to break down any lingering ethnocentrism or chauvinism among Westerners and make them less inclined to resist the mass migration of non-Christian non-Europeans into Western Europe and North America.

Yet these claims only tend to make matters worse, for they raise an uncomfortable question: if Islamic civilization was so advanced during the Abbasid caliphate, or at any other time, what happened? Why didn't it continue to grow and develop? Why did Europe instead surpass it and spread its culture and values around the world?

The excuses at this point grow numerous: it wasn't because of any superiority of European culture or civilization, it was simply because the Europeans were better armed, achieving their superiority through brute force and even genocide. Then their racism and colonialism impeded the development of non-Christian, non-European cultures. These claims ignore the colonialism of the Islamic world during the period of the caliphates, as well as the efforts of the Western colonials to build up, rather than solely to exploit, the indigenous people in the lands they colonized.

Also, given the Qur'an's call to fight unbelievers until "religion is all for Allah" (8:39), there can be little doubt that if the Abbasids and Ottomans had been able, they would have been every bit as energetic in colonization and imperialism as the Europeans were later, and in light of the status of non-Muslims in Islamic societies, much more ruthless.

Nevertheless, for the weathervane of the zeitgeist that is GeoHussar, not only were the Abbasids highly educated, they were also tolerant to a degree that puts Europeans to shame:

"Another huge similarity between New York City and Baghdad was that they had a large Jewish population that actually lived in safety, while Christian Europe was massacring or force-converting Jewish populations left and right, and the Byzantine Empire was doing it on a slightly less horrifying level. The Jewish population got to coexist with Christians, Muslims, and anyone of any other faith, as long as they paid what the jizya, the tax." This ignores the institutionalized discrimination that went along with paying the *jizya*, and the precarious existence that the dhimmis lived, as their lives could be taken at any time if their Muslim overlords judged that they had violated the terms of their "contract of protection." It likewise leads to an unwelcome question: why did truly tolerant and pluralistic societies develop only in the West, while Muslim-majority countries such as Pakistan and Egypt are notorious for their intolerance and ongoing harassment of religious minorities?

Islamic law codifies that intolerance. The treatment of religious minorities is based on the Qur'an, which mandates that they manifest "willing submission" to the Muslims and "feel themselves subdued." (9:29)

A CAPRICIOUS GOD

Islam also contains within it the seeds of its own intellectual failure. This is what Pope Benedict XVI was addressing in Regensburg, Germany on September 12, 2006, when he delivered a speech that quickly became notorious after Muslims around the world rioted and even killed innocent people because Benedict had supposedly insulted Muhammad.

The pope was quoting the fourteenth-century Roman Emperor Manuel II Palaiologos, who said: "Show me just what

Muhammad brought that was new, and there you will find things only evil and inhuman, such as his command to spread by the sword the faith he preached.... God is not pleased by blood—and not acting reasonably is contrary to God's nature. Faith is born of the soul, not the body. Whoever would lead someone to faith needs the ability to speak well and to reason properly, without violence and threats.... To convince a reasonable soul, one does not need a strong arm, or weapons of any kind, or any other means of threatening a person with death."[237]

Pope Benedict was dismayed over the Muslim reaction to this, as he had only intended to delineate some differences between Islam and Christianity. He had meant to focus not so much on Manuel II Palaiologos' criticism of Muhammad, but upon the emperor's statement that "not acting reasonably is contrary to God's nature." The pope's point was that in Islam, nothing could be said to be "contrary to God's nature." Benedict observed that "for Muslim teaching, God is absolutely transcendent. His will is not bound up with any of our categories, even that of rationality."[238]

Although this was absolutely true, it annoyed many Muslim authorities. One hundred of those authorities replied with an Open Letter to the pope, explaining to him what they thought he had failed to grasp. To refute this idea that Islam envisioned "a capricious God who might or might not command us to evil,"[239] they presented a series of quotations from the Qur'an, describing

---

237 Pope Benedict XVI, "Faith, reason and the university: memories and reflections," Papal Address at University of Regensburg, September 12, 2006, https://www.vatican.va/content/benedict-xvi/en/speeches/2006/september/documents/hf_ben-xvi_spe_20060912_university-regensburg.html. Accessed October 30, 2024.

238 Ibid.

239 Muslim Religious Leaders, "Open Letter to His Holiness Pope Benedict XVI," Islamica Magazine, 2006, https://www.catholicculture.org/culture/library/view.cfm?recnum=7910. Accessed September 20, 2024.

Allah as one who "enjoins justice and kindness" and is, as every chapter of the Qur'an except one affirms, the compassionate, the merciful:

> To say that for Muslims 'God's Will is not bound up in any of our categories' is also a simplification which may lead to a misunderstanding. God has many Names in Islam, including the Merciful, the Just, the Seeing, the Hearing, the Knowing, the Loving, and the Gentle.... As this concerns His Will, to conclude that Muslims believe in a capricious God who might or might not command us to evil is to forget that God says in the Qur'an, *Lo! God enjoins justice and kindness, and giving to kinsfolk, and forbids lewdness and abomination and wickedness. He exhorts you in order that ye may take heed* (al-Nahl, 16:90). Equally, it is to forget that God says in the Qur'an that *He has prescribed for Himself mercy* (al-An'am, 6:12; see also 6:54), and that God says in the Qur'an, *My Mercy encompasses everything* (al-A'raf 7:156). The word for mercy, *rahmah,* can also be translated as love, kindness, and compassion. From this word *rahmah* comes the sacred formula Muslims use daily, *In the Name of God, the Merciful, the Compassionate.* Is it not self-evident that spilling innocent blood goes against mercy and compassion?[240]

[240] Ibid.

This did not, however, address the point that Pope Benedict was actually making. When he asserted that Allah's "will is not bound up with any of our categories," and quoted the Islamic scholar Ibn Hazm's startling statement that "were it God's will, we would even have to practise idolatry," the pope did not mean that Allah might command his people to do evil.[241] Rather, Benedict's point was that Allah might alter the meaning of what it meant to do good or evil. Then Muslims would do evil, thinking it was good, as the Old Testament prophet Isaiah had warned against (Isaiah 5:20). To assert otherwise, that Allah was bound to maintain the same definitions of good and evil at all times, would be to limit his absolute transcendence.

The idea that Allah was absolute transcendent and thus could not be expected to do anything the same way twice lessened interest among Muslims in observing the movement of the heavenly bodies. Allah could change them tomorrow. Astronomy and the attendant sciences were thus left to develop in the West, not in the Islamic world.

Eight hundred years before Benedict XVI became pope, the renowned Jewish philosopher Moses Maimonides (1135–1204) stated essentially the same thing about Muslim scientists:

> Human intellect does not perceive any reason why a body should be in a certain place instead of being in another. In the same manner they say that reason admits the possibility that an existing being should be larger or smaller than it really is, or that it should be different in form and position from what it really is; e.g., a man

[241] Benedict XVI, op. cit.

might have the height of a mountain, might have several heads, and fly in the air; or an elephant might be as small as an insect, or an insect as huge as an elephant.

This method of admitting possibilities is applied to the whole Universe. Whenever they affirm that a thing belongs to this class of admitted possibilities, they say that it can have this form and that it is also possible that it be found differently, and that the one form is not more possible than the other; but they do not ask whether the reality confirms their assumption. They say that the thing which exists with certain constant and permanent forms, dimensions, and properties, only follows the direction of habit, just as the king generally rides on horseback through the streets of the city, and is never found departing from this habit; but reason does not find it impossible that he should walk on foot through the place: there is no doubt that he may do so, and this possibility is fully admitted by the intellect.

Similarly, earth moves towards the centre, fire turns away from the centre; fire causes heat, water causes cold, in accordance with a certain habit; but it is logically not impossible that a deviation from this habit should occur, namely, that fire should cause cold, move downward, and still be fire; that the water should cause

> heat, move upward, and still be water. On this foundation their whole fabric is constructed.[242]

Maimonides provides a simple summation of why science did not develop in the Islamic world. The Qur'an even states it plainly: "He cannot be questioned about what he does." (21:23) Allah cannot be questioned not only because to interrogate him would be an unacceptable manifestation of effrontery, but because what he does, how he orders the universe, could change radically from moment to moment. Why, then, waste any time trying to figure out how it all works?

In contrast, the Bible envisions a universe constructed according to consistent and observable laws: "If you can break my covenant with the day and my covenant with the night, so that day and night will not come at their appointed time, then also my covenant with David my servant may be broken, so that he shall not have a son to reign on his throne..." (Jeremiah 33:20–21). God has "fixed all the bounds of the earth" (Psalm 74:17). This expectation of consistency formed the basis for modern science. Without it, Islam could not, and did not, develop the same desire to understand the workings of the world, and the universe.

[242] Moses Maimonides, The Guide for the Perplexed, M. Friedländer, trans., (New York: Barnes & Noble, 2004).

CHAPTER TWELVE

THE FICTIONAL PALACE OF ISLAMIC ACHIEVEMENTS

INVENTING THE PAST

If Islam had no glorious intellectual past, or not one that could seriously be compared to the intellectual development of the Christian West, then one would have to be invented. The noted twentieth-century historian of the Arabs, Philip K. Hitti, showed himself to be a more sophisticated version of the TikToker GeoHussar when he wrote, "For while [the Caliphs] al-Rashid [786–809] and al-Mamun [813–833] were delving into Greek and Persian philosophy, their contemporaries in the West, Charlemagne and his lords, were reportedly dabbling in the art of writing their names.... No people in the early Middle Ages contributed to human progress as much as did the Arabs."[243]

[243] Philip K. Hitti, The Arabs: A Short History (Washington, DC: Regnery Publishing, 1996), 120, 5.

Here again, while such talk appealed to contemporary Western self-hatred, it just led one to ask why the Arabs were so backward and impoverished before they struck oil. Even worse for Hitti and others who would have taken what he said as patently obvious, it wasn't true.

Numerous similar myths have taken hold in the popular imagination. In November 2002, a man named Jassim Amiri repeated one of them in a letter to Forbes magazine: "The most important invention of all time," Amiri wrote, "was 'zero'.... When the Muslims invented the zero, they had no idea that it, along with the number one would be running nearly everything the mankind needs in the centuries ahead."[244] Yet "the Muslims" did not invent the zero. The concept of the zero emerged around the fourth century BC; the only role Muslims had in it was that the Muslim mathematician Mohammed ibn-Musa al-Khowarizmi began in the eighth century to use the modern symbol to denote it.[245]

Many people, meanwhile, make a great deal out of the apparent fact that Muslims preserved the works of the ancient Greek philosophers, translating them into Arabic from which they were much later translated into Western European languages. In reality, however, the people who actually did this translating work were not Muslims at all. The fifth century Christian priest Probus of Antioch, not any Muslim scholar, first introduced Aristotle into what came to be known as the Middle East, centuries before the advent of Islam.[246] Huneyn ibn-Ishaq (809–873), who was also a Christian, spent years translating works of Aristotle, Galen, Plato

---

244 Letters to Forbes.com, November 15, 2002, https://www.forbes.com/letters/02/1115.shtml, accessed October 9, 2024.

245 "Who Invented the Zero?," History.com, June 6, 2023, https://www.history.com/news/who-invented-the-zero, accessed October 9, 2024.

246 Caesar E. Farah, Islam, Sixth Edition (Hauppauge, New York: Barrons, 2000), 198.

and Hippocrates into Syriac; they were translated into Arabic from Huneyn's Syriac editions.[247]

SHOWCASING FAKE MUSLIM ACHIEVEMENTS

In the absence of actual achievements, enter the Western public relations machine, itself an invention of non-Muslims. Ever ready to demonstrate their own historical and cultural inferiority and the superiority and supremacy of Islam, Western non-Muslims have never hesitated to join Islamic apologists in constructing fictional palaces of Islamic achievements.

One example is "1001 Inventions," which states proudly that it is "an award-winning UK science and cultural heritage organisation"[248] which "has engaged over 500 million people through a network of strategic partnerships including governments, corporates as well as educational, cultural and international organisations such as World Food Programme (WFP), UNESCO and National Geographic."[249] Other non-Muslim organizations that have given 1001 Inventions a lavish welcome all over the Western world include Google Arts & Culture, the World Bank Global Partnership for Youth in Development, the BBC, the British government's Home Office, the Discovery Channel, the History Channel, the New York Academy of Sciences, and the publisher Random House.[250]

1001 Inventions is so popular with the Western intelligentsia because it "leverages on the power of storytelling, interlinking

247 Elias B. Skaff, The Place of the Patriarchs of Antioch in Church History (Newton Centre, Massachusetts: Sophia Press, 1993), 169.

248 1001 Inventions, http://www.1001inventions.com/, accessed October 9, 2024.

249 "1001 Inventions Global Partners," 1001 Inventions, https://www.1001inventions.com/about/credits/, accessed October 10, 2024.

250 Ibid.

themes of science, history and culture, to disrupt the notion of STEM [science, technology, engineering and mathematics] being exclusive."[251] To that end, "1001 Inventions productions uncover fascinating historical contributions of lesser-known pioneers from Arab, Asian and other Eastern cultures. This helps young people understand that each one of them has an equal opportunity to become the scientist of the future. Such inclusive content helps promote harmony, respect and tolerance."[252]

Who could object to such a noble endeavor? Yet it carries an edge of sadness, for the promise of equal opportunity was based on a clever and complex web of wild exaggerations and outright fictions. It might have been enough to state that the UK affirmed equality of rights for all people, and thus that Muslim and Arab children had just as much of an opportunity to work in scientific and technological fields as everyone else, but instead, in order to foster both admiration for Islam and grand aspirations among Muslim youth, 1001 Inventions created a mythic Islamic past—glorious, but no less mythic for all that.

1001 Inventions began in 2005 as "a unique UK based educational project that reveals the rich heritage that the Muslim community share with other communities in the UK and Europe."[253] It was "a non-religious and non-political project seeking to allow the positive aspects of progress in science and technology to act as a bridge in understanding the interdependence of communities throughout human history."[254]

---

[251] "Mission and Purpose," 1001 Inventions, https://www.1001inventions.com/about/mission-and-purpose/, accessed October 9, 2024.

[252] Ibid.

[253] "Discover the Muslim heritage in our World," MuslimHeritage.com, https://muslimheritage.com/1001/, accessed October 9, 2024.

[254] Ibid.

Yet for all the financial and cultural firepower behind it, the entire 1001 Inventions endeavor is shot through with distortions, exaggerations, wishful thinking and worse. Aaron Adair, an academic who has looked closely at the traveling 1001 Inventions exhibit and accompanying popular book (published in tandem with National Geographic) observes that "there is really a misnomer in the entire premise. All the innovations mentioned are called 'Muslim' or 'Islamic', but that is rather odd. For one thing, there is very little cited to show that it was the religion of these inventors/discoverers that made their work possible."[255] Thus while the inventions in question may or may not have actually come from Muslims, they were not products of their Islamic faith.

Adair continues by noting that, as in the case of Probus of Antioch noted above, "a fair number of the people in question were not Muslim, nor were many of the scientists working under the various caliphates. It would be much more accurate to not talk about an Islamic Golden Age of science, but of an Arab Golden Age. The language was Arabic, used by Jews, Christians, Muslims, and pagans, which binds together all this work.... So making all the innovations done during a time when Islam was dominant rather confuses the issue."[256]

Even worse, he notes that the *1001 Inventions* book takes immense liberties to make its case: "In its section about lunar formations, it does not talk about Arab discussion about the moon and its features, but instead about the various features on the moon *named* after Arab scientists by Europeans that discovered those formations. The Muslim invention here is actually

255 Aaron Adair, "1001 Inventions from Medieval Muslim?," Finding Nergal, Seeking Stars, November 15, 2012. https://gilgamesh42.wordpress.com/2012/11/15/1001-inventions-from-medieval-muslim/, accessed October 10, 2024.

256 Ibid.

European!"[257] Thus the vaunted treasury of Muslim achievements becomes nothing more than a partial chronicle of how non-Muslim Westerners paid tribute to Muslims who supposedly paved the way for their modern-day achievements.

Even the exploits of those alleged forerunners are shrouded in legend. The *1001 Inventions* book describes the invention of one Abbas ibn Firnas, who was supposedly the first person to construct a viable flying machine and take to the air in the year 852:

> In the Rusafa area on the outskirts of Cordoba, Ibn Firnas mounted a hill and appeared before the crowd in his bird costume, made from silk covered with eagle feathers.... [He] explained with a piece of paper how he planned to fly using the wings fitted on his arms: "Presently, I shall take leave of you. By guiding these wings up and down, I should ascend like the birds. If all goes well, after soaring for a time I should be able to return safely to your side."
>
> He flew to a significant height and hung in the air for more than ten minutes before plummeting to the ground, breaking the wings and one of his vertebrae.[258]

Impressive indeed, as this is supposed to have happened in the ninth century, over a millennium before Wilbur and Orville Wright successfully tested their flying machine on the beach at

[257] Ibid.

[258] Salim T.S. Al-Hassani, 1001 Inventions: The Enduring Legacy of Muslim Civilization: Official Companion to the 1001 Inventions Exhibition, 3rd edition (Washington, DC: National Geographic, 2012), 297.

Kitty Hawk, North Carolina. Thus again the problem arises: if Abbas Ibn Firnas really mounted a successful flight, why didn't the Islamic world continue to produce pioneers of aviation? Why did air travel only become common due to innovations made in the twentieth-century West?

Adair points out more:

> What is described here is a powered flight. Ascending like a bird, flying for 10 minutes before plummeting, guiding wings up and down, returning to the starting point (or at least attempting to). And over and over again, the authors of *1001 Inventions* call the wings of Ibn Firnas a "flying machine." This description is like someone trying to flap their arms and successfully flying this way. And this is impossible. Humans don't have the build to flap their arms and hold themselves up (at least on Earth; it might work on Titan!). This is not supported by the sources I have mentioned above (and Muslim Heritage has nothing to support that either), and it doesn't fit what we know about history or physiology. Quite simply, this has as much plausibility as *Dumbo*.[259]

Even that is not all. The principal source for any information about Ibn Firnas' flight is a Muslim chronicler, Ahmed Mohammad al-Maqqari, who wrote about this first flight around seven hundred years after it is supposed to have happened. Was al-Maqqari repeating soberly recorded historical fact, or passing

259 Aaron Adair, "Ibn Firnas Flies Again — More Trouble with 1001 Inventions," Finding Nergal, Seeking Stars, November 17, 2012. https://gilgamesh42.wordpress.com/2012/11/17/ibn-firnas-flies-again/ Accessed October 10, 2024.

on a good story that had undergone considerable embellishment, or may even have been entirely fictional? There is no way to tell, but either way, his account differs considerably from that of *1001 Inventions*. Al-Maqqari wrote:

> Abú-l-'abbás Kasim Ibn Firnas, the physician, was the first who made glass out of clay, and who established fabrics of it in Andalus.... Among other very curious experiments which he made, one is his trying to fly. He covered himself with feathers for the purpose, attached a couple of wings to his body, and, getting on an eminence, flung himself down into the air, when, according to the testimony of several trustworthy writers who witnessed the performance, he flew to a considerable distance, as if he had been a bird, but in alighting again on the place whence he had started his back was very much hurt, for not knowing that birds when they alight come down upon their tails, he forgot to provide himself with one.[260]

There is nothing in al-Maqqari's account about Ibn Firnas staying aloft for ten minutes. Nor is there anything about his guiding his wings up and down in order to prolong his time in the air. The crowning difficulty with taking any of this seriously comes when al-Maqqari adds that Ibn Firnas constructed a realistic and accurate design of the heavens in his home, and claimed to have seen Muhammad himself, although it is unclear whether

260 Ibid.

or not he meant that he saw him in a glimpse of paradise when he was flying around right underneath the heavenly realms:

> The following verse is the composition of Ibn Firnas himself, who addressed it to the Amir Mohammed. "I saw the Prince of the believers, Mohammed, and the flourishing star of benevolence shone bright upon his countenance." To which Mumen replied, when he was told of it, "Yes, thou art right, but it vanished the very moment thou didst come near it…"[261]

If Ibn Firnas is saying that he saw Muhammad while he was flying in his makeshift flying machine, that would only underscore the legendary character of the whole story.

The 1001 Inventions website states that that "some people unaware of what was accomplished during Muslim civilisation believe that astronomy died with the Greeks, and was brought to life again by Nicolas Copernicus, the fifteenth-century Polish astronomer who is famous for introducing the sun-centered theory of the solar system, which marked the beginning of modern astronomy—even though it was not universally accepted."[262] Instead, 1001 Inventions asserts that heliocentrism originated with a Muslim: "However, many historians now think it is not a coincidence that his geometrical models for the Sun, Moon, and five naked-eye planets are identical to those prepared by Ibn al-Shatir more than a century before him."[263]

---

261 Ibid.

262 "The Birth of Modern Astronomy," 1001 Inventions, https://www.1001inventions.com/to-modern-astronomy/, accessed October 10, 2024.

263 Ibid.

Why, then, is Copernicus, rather than al-Shatir, revered as the father of modern astronomy? Can this be ascribed solely to the West's cultural imperialism? Or did al-Shatir's alleged discoveries remain unexamined in the Islamic world, so that it fell to Copernicus to build upon them in the West? If the failure of Muslims to build upon the work of al-Shatir and so many others can be ascribed to colonialism and imperialism, and yet Islam contains within it the impetus to create a civilization far superior to that of the West, why has the Islamic world not been able to shake off the baneful effects of the West's supposed interference and exploitation?

Meanwhile, why are some of the pivotal institutions in the Western world so eager to showcase this farrago of exaggeration and fantasy? Why is asking the questions that exercises such as 1001 Inventions raise, about why the Islamic world's many alleged inventions came to little or nothing until Westerners took them up later, dismissed out of hand as "Islamophobic"?

Despite the wishful thinking and illogic at the heart of this endeavor, the idea that the Islamic world far outstripped the West culturally and intellectually in the past and could easily do so again took hold in the popular mind, largely due to the relentless propagation of the fantasy world of 1001 Inventions and other endeavors like it. In October 2008, the *Telegraph* reported that Britain's schools minister, Jim Knight, "claimed lessons in the scientific and cultural innovations of Islam over the centuries would give young Muslims a sense of worth and reduce their risk of becoming alienated and falling under the spell of radicals."[264] We can see in the

[264] Martin Beckford, "Teach children what Muslims did for us, says minister Jim Knight," Telegraph, October 17, 2008, https://www.telegraph.co.uk/education/3209469/Teach-children-what-Muslims-did-for-us-says-minister-Jim-Knight.html. Accessed October 30, 2024.

intervening years how well that worked. Oblivious to what was to come, however, Knight "said it could also bring divided communities closer together, by teaching children from other backgrounds about the debt we all owe to Muslims—from coffee and pinhole cameras to the three-course dinner and advancements in maths."

Coffee? Pinhole cameras? The three-course dinner? Again, even if these did originate among Muslims or Arabs, there is nothing specifically Islamic about them. Nor is there anything about Islam that led people to discover coffee or decide to serve dinner in three courses. Yet as pathetic as these claims are, and as poorly as they reflect upon Islam and the Islamic world for having such a paucity of achievements that all they can show for themselves is a cup of coffee and a dessert, Jim Knight comes out looking the worst of all. Did he actually believe that propagating these alleged achievements would ease relations between Muslims and non-Muslims in Britain? Did he really think that native Britons would shrug off rising crime, rape gang activity, and jihad violence, by reminding themselves that Muslims invented coffee?

Knight's surname suggested a nobler past. Almost a millennium ago, his forefathers may have been among those who traversed Europe to protect Christian lands from further jihadi encroachment. They understood the challenge that Islam posed to their societies and were prepared to meet it. At the sad modern end of this bloodline, however, a Knight looked at the same threat and thought that he could stave it off by reminding his people of the glorious achievements of the invaders, which were largely exaggerated or altogether illusory.

Yet Western governments were and are wholly committed to this project. In the summer of 2010, Barack Obama even directed Charlie Bolden, whom he had placed in charge of the National Aeronautics and Space Administration (NASA), to prioritize not space exploration but the glorification of alleged Muslim achievements: "Perhaps foremost, [Obama] wanted me to find a way to reach out to the Muslim world and engage much more with predominantly Muslim nations to help them feel good about their historic contribution to science, math, and engineering."[265]

[265] Keith Cowing, "Charlie Bolden: Stealth Middle East Diplomat?," NASA Watch, July 2, 2010, https://nasawatch.com/uncategorized/charlie-bolden-stealth-middle-east-diplomat/. Accessed October 30, 2024.

CHAPTER THIRTEEN

ADOPTING ISLAMIC GRIEVANCES

FIGHTING FOR LIBERATION OF PALESTINE...AND TURTLE ISLAND

Ever eager to be helpful and "build bridges," leftist non-Muslims have also readily joined forces with Muslims, even when the latter are engaged in advancing the jihad that would ultimately turn against those non-Muslim allies as well as everyone else.

Students for Justice in Palestine (SJP), which has been frequently accused of antisemitism, and Jewish Voice for Peace (JVP) might appear at first glance to be strange bedfellows. They are, however, united in their leftism, which includes a shared hatred for Israel. The very existence of Israel, as the world's only Jewish state, is a standing rebuke to the left's drive for collectivization and uniformity. And so in the aftermath of Hamas' October 7, 2023, jihad massacre in Israel, the SJP and the JVP emerged as the two most active and strident pro-Hamas groups on college and university campuses nationwide, united in their hatred.

After October 7, the open support for Hamas on American campuses shocked the nation and the world, and demonstrated one of the bitter fruits of the left's takeover of academia in the US. At the University of North Carolina at Chapel Hill, one student proclaimed: "All of us are Hamas."[266] At Harvard, students greeted the news of the Hamas massacre by publishing a statement that placed the blame for the violence solely on Israel.[267] All over the nation, college and university students demonstrated in favor of the Palestinians, without bothering to issue even the weakest and most pro-forma condemnation of Hamas. On some campuses, Jewish students were menaced and even attacked.[268]

Students for Justice in Palestine has no national organization, but it does have a national website enunciating its motives and goals. The National Students for Justice in Palestine site states that it is "supporting over two hundred Palestine solidarity organizations across occupied Turtle Island, we aim to develop a student movement that is connected, disciplined, and equipped with the tools necessary achieve Palestinian liberation."[269]

"Occupied Turtle Island" refers to North America. Turtle Island is a name for the continent taken from Native American folklore, and of course it is "occupied" today by the evil white oppressors who are, in SJP's view, also responsible for the supposed

---

266 Yoni Michanie (@Yoni Michanie), Twitter/X, October 14, 2023, https://twitter.com/YoniMichanie/status/1713194179499524286. Accessed October 30, 2024.

267 Yael Bar tur (@yaelbt), Twitter/X, October 8, 2023, https://twitter.com/yaelbt/status/1710875529249792487. Accessed October 30, 2024.

268 Melissa Koenig and Jorge Fitz-Gibbon, "Harvard student mobbed by pro-Palestinian demonstrators yelling 'shame' on campus: video," New York Post, November 1, 2023, https://nypost.com/2023/11/01/news/harvard-student-mobbed-by-pro-palestinian-demonstrators-on-campus-video/. Accessed October 30, 2024. Haley Cohen, "Pro-Palestinian protesters assault several Jewish students at Tulane, witnesses say," Jewish Insider, October 27, 2023, https://jewishinsider.com/2023/10/pro-palestinian-protesters-assault-several-jewish-students-at-tulane-2/. Accessed October 30, 2024.

269 National Students For Justice In Palestine, https://nationalsjp.org/. Accessed October 30, 2024.

occupation and oppression of Palestinians. As absurd as this locution is—in light of the fact that no one aside from woke millennial leftists, not even Native Americans themselves, refers to North America as "Turtle Island"—the National SJP website uses the term consistently and without irony. It invites visitors to the site to "learn more about recent victories in the Boycott, Divestment, and Sanctions (BDS) movement on campuses across Turtle Island, and beyond!"[270]

OCCUPIED PALESTINE

The site speaks more frequently and thoroughly about another land that exists only in fantasy and propaganda, although in this case that propaganda has been far more successful and is much more pervasive today: occupied Palestine. Despite the fact that no independent state of Palestine ever existed in history, and that the Palestinian nationality is an invention dating from the 1960s, the National SJP website maintains the fiction that it represents an endeavor to liberate an oppressed people, which is to state a jihad imperative in the language of the left. It traces the origins of "the student movement for the liberation of Palestine" to the 1950s, saying that it began with "the formation of the General Union of Palestinian Students (GUPS)."[271]

This statement contains a small but telling inaccuracy. GUPS was actually known as the General Union of Palestine Students (GUPS).[272] When it was founded, "Palestine" referred to the region where the state of Israel was located, but no one considered

[270] Ibid.

[271] Ibid.

[272] General Union of Palestine Students, https://web.archive.org/web/20190702185159/http://www.gups.org/. Accessed October 30, 2024.

the Levantine Arabs who lived there along with the Jews to be distinct ethnically, linguistically, culturally or religiously from the other Arabs of the region. There was as yet no "Palestinian" nationality, and would not be until the 1960s, when it was invented by the KGB and Yasir Arafat as a rhetorical weapon to use against Israel.

In a 1977 interview with the Dutch newspaper *Trouw*, PLO executive committee member Zahir Muhsein acknowledged that the Palestinian people were a propaganda invention:

> The Palestinian people does not exist. The creation of a Palestinian state is only a means for continuing our struggle against the state of Israel for our Arab unity. In reality today there is no difference between Jordanians, Palestinians, Syrians and Lebanese. Only for political and tactical reasons do we speak today about the existence of a Palestinian people, since Arab national interests demand that we posit the existence of a distinct "Palestinian people" to oppose Zionism.
>
> For tactical reasons, Jordan, which is a sovereign state with defined borders, cannot raise claims to Haifa and Jaffa, while as a Palestinian, I can undoubtedly demand Haifa, Jaffa, Beer-Sheva and Jerusalem. However, the moment we reclaim our right to all of Palestine, we will not wait even a minute to unite Palestine and Jordan.[273]

[273] James Dorsey, "Wij zijn alleen Palestijn om politieke redden," Trouw, March 31, 1977, quoted in Robert Spencer, The Palestinian Delusion: The Catastrophic History of the Middle East Peace Process (New York: Bombardier Books, 2019), 95-6.

Abdul Hamid Sharif, the Prime Minister of Jordan, said in 1980, "The Palestinians and Jordanians do not belong to different nationalities. They hold the same Jordanian passports, are Arabs and have the same Jordanian culture."[274] King Hussein of Jordan put it most succinctly of all in 1981: "The truth is that Jordan is Palestine and Palestine is Jordan."[275]

The SJP, however, is dedicated to the "liberation" of this contrived, fictional land, because that "liberation" will destroy Israel. Accordingly, the National SJP site appropriates GUPS into its pseudohistorical scenario: "From the U.S. to Palestine, GUPS chapters galvanized thousands of students towards a liberated Palestine."[276] That led to an even greater movement: "The '90s wave of corrupt politicians and faulty deals changed the liberation movement as we knew it and many institutions, including the student movement, collapsed. In the absence of a Palestinan [sic] student movement, organizations such as Students for Justice in Palestine emerged across occupied Turtle Island (U.S. and Canada) as a way to educate, advocate, and mobilize in support for Palestinian liberation."[277]

Why there was no Palestinian student movement decades after GUPS had begun galvanizing "thousands of students towards a liberated Palestine" is left unexplained. It is noteworthy, however, that the SJP traces its own origins to "faulty deals" of the 1990s, which is apparently a reference to the Oslo Accords that were meant to establish a framework for the establishment of a

274 Lior Ben-Ami, "What is Palestine? Who are the Palestinians? Whose land is it anyway?," MidEastTruth.com, October 18, 2016, https://mideasttruth.com/forum/viewtopic.php?t=12097. Accessed October 30, 2024.

275 Ibid.

276 "Our Purpose," National Students For Justice In Palestine, https://nationalsjp.org/about. Accessed October 30, 2024.

277 Ibid.

Palestinian state that would recognize Israel's right to exist and live peacefully next to the Jewish state. While most people today continue to assume that the Israeli-Palestinian conflict would be ended if the Palestinians were granted a state, SJP here reveals obliquely what it makes abundantly clear in its campus activism: it is not interested in seeing the founding of a Palestinian state that will coexist with Israel. Rather, like Hamas, it wants to see Israel altogether destroyed.

FOUNDED BY A PROFESSOR OF "ISLAMOPHOBIA"

In pursuit of that goal, SJP was founded at the University of California Berkeley in October 2000. It is the brainchild of Hatem Bazian, whom the Berkeley Center for Race and Gender notes is a "Continuing Lecturer, Chair and Founder, CRG's Islamophobia Research and Documentation Project."[278] He is also "a co-founder and Professor of Islamic Law and Theology at Zaytuna College, the 1st Accredited Muslim Liberal Arts College in the United States. In addition, Prof. Bazian is a lecturer in the Departments of Near Eastern and Asian American and Asian Diaspora Studies at the University of California, Berkeley."[279]

Besides SJP, Bazian is also the founder of an organization called American Muslims for Palestine (AMP), which has likewise been accused of antisemitism but nevertheless enjoys mainstream respectability, and has hosted the vociferously anti-Israel Reps. Rashida Tlaib (D-Michigan) and Ilhan Omar (D-Minnesota) as featured speakers.

278 "Hatem Bazian," Berkeley Center for Race and Gender, https://crg.berkeley.edu/people/hatem-bazian. Accessed October 30, 2024.

279 Ibid.

IPT News reported in May 2017 that AMP was set up as a "ruse" by former officials of the Islamic Association for Palestine (IAP) and the American Muslim Society (AMS) after those two organizations were "found liable for an American teen's death in a 1996 terrorist attack" and ceased operations, claiming to be unable to pay.[280] *IPT* adds, "A subsequent criminal prosecution found that other defendants in the original lawsuit, like the Holy Land Foundation for Relief and Development (HLF) and the United Association for Studies and Research, were part of a Muslim Brotherhood-created Hamas-support network in the United States called the Palestine Committee."[281]

Even the ADL, which has largely morphed into a smear group targeting pro-Israel advocates who aren't far enough to the left for the organization's taste, noted that the AMP "promotes extreme anti-Israel views and has at times provided a platform for anti-Semitism under the guise of educating Americans about 'the just cause of Palestine and the rights of self-determination.'"[282]

Despite all this, Tlaib was featured as the guest of honor at AMP's December 2019 national convention, and has spoken at other AMP events as well. Fox News reported in 2021 that Tlaib and Omar "were featured as speakers for a virtual AMP event in November 2020, and both congresswomen attended the same pro-Palestine conference as Bazian."[283]

If Rashida Tlaib were an America-First patriot and had an associate so multiply linked to hatred and violence as Hatem

---

280 "Lawsuit Targets American Muslims for Palestine," IPT News, May 12, 2017, https://www.investigativeproject.org/6123/lawsuit-targets-american-muslims-for-palestine. Accessed October 30, 2024.

281 Ibid.

282 Ibid.

283 Houston Keene, "Tlaib ally runs organization accused of promoting anti-Semitism," Fox News, June 2, 2021, https://www.foxnews.com/politics/tlaib-donor-uc-berkeley-prof-runs-org-adl-said-preaches-anti-semitism-under-guise. Accessed October 30, 2024.

Bazian, she would have been hounded out of Congress long ago, but these kinds of associations are just fine with the political and media establishment. And in these days of a thoroughly corrupted and politicized academic environment, Bazian has all the respectable bona fides. As a professor who researches "Islamophobia," he taps into the left's current obsession with race and victimhood, as well as its hatred and contempt for Western intellectual and religious traditions.

Researching and documenting "Islamophobia" doesn't mean that Bazian keeps track of people who attack or harass innocent Muslims. Instead, Bazian is essentially a professor of Sharia enforcement: he uses the smear propaganda term "Islamophobia" to stigmatize those who dare to note how Islamic jihadis use the texts and teachings of Islam to justify violence and make recruits among peaceful Muslims. Anyone who notices that the jihadis' motivating ideology is Islamic to the core has already been or soon will be added to Bazian's list of "Islamophobes"; the objective is to make everyone too frightened of this stigmatization to speak out, so that jihad can advance unopposed and unimpeded.

Bazian has engaged in other kinds of thuggery as well. He has openly called for an *intifada*, a violent uprising, in the United States as well as in Israel,[284] and regarding supporters of Israel, he has declared: "We need to harass them."[285]

In a sane society, Hatem Bazian would at very least be under investigation for ties to jihad terror activity. Instead, he is a respected professor at a prestigious university, and a close associate of an influential member of the House of Representatives.

---

284 Robert Spencer, "UC Berkeley lecturer calls for an intifada in the United States," Jihad Watch, April 12, 2004, https://jihadwatch.org/2004/04/uc-berkeley-lecturer-calls-for-an-intifada-in-the-united-states. Accessed October 30, 2024.

285 Canary Mission, "The Most Dangerous Professor in America?," YouTube video, July 12, 2017, https://www.youtube.com/watch?v=Y2k5QaUOBE4. Accessed October 30, 2024.

He is thus a prime example of how our academic institutions have lost their way, deserve no public funding, and are in radical need of reform. But as the presence of his friend Tlaib in Congress shows, those who would take needed action against our corrupted universities and colleges are themselves just as compromised.

A LOOSE ORGANIZATION

Bazian is the founder of the SJP, but he is not its national director. There is no such person; the national organization does not exercise a coordinating role. NGO Monitor reported in 2015 that "as an organization, SJP exists without an apparent central leadership or central structural framework. Each SJP chapter operates independently and is responsible for forming its own constitutions, finding funding sources, and organizing activities. Indeed, several SJP chapters, such as Palestine Solidarity Committee at Harvard College and Students United for Palestinian Equal Rights at Washington University do not actually carry the name Students for Justice in Palestine. However, SJP has developed regional networks to aid in coordinating campaigns across several campuses, hinting at greater consolidation."[286]

The SJP has enjoyed noteworthy success. The National SJP website looks back with satisfaction on the years since the organization was founded. "Nearly two decades," it still says in December 2023, which was actually over twenty-three years after the SJP was founded, "after the formation of the first Students for Justice in Palestine, the movement for Palestine has taken colleges and

[286] Yona A. Schiffmiller, "BDS on American Campuses: SJP and its NGO Network," NGO Monitor, 2015, https://ngo-monitor.org/reports/bds_on_american_campuses_sjp_and_its_ngo_network/. Accessed October 30, 2024.

universities across North America by storm. With over 200 campus Palestine solidarity organizations across the continent, students have been leaders in uplifting demands for freedom, justice, and equality for the Palestinian people."[287]

Bazian's SJP is also largely responsible for the current affinity for Hamas among campus leftists. SJP chapters have described Hamas in terms that make it appear to be a benign humanitarian organization:

> Hamas (the Movement of Islamic Resistance) was founded in 1987 during the first Palestinian intifada along religious-nationalist ideological lines. A vast social organization, Hamas provides schools, medical care, and day care for a number of Palestinians who otherwise live difficult lives. Hamas also has a militia established to fight Israeli troops in the occupied territories, and has turned out to be a counterweight to Fatah, given its long record of opposition to the Oslo Accords and its clean record as far as domestic corruption in governance was concerned. Democratically elected, Hamas officials have often stated that they are ready for a long-term truce with Israel during which time final status negotiations can occur.[288]

It is not surprising that these indoctrinated and miseducated students would turn out in force on behalf of a "vast social

---

287 "Our Purpose," National Students For Justice In Palestine, op. cit.

288 "Campus BDS Fail: UCSD votes down divestment attempt," Elder of Ziyon, March 1, 2012, https://elderofziyon.blogspot.com/2012/03/campus-bds-fail-ucsd-votes-down.html. Accessed October 30, 2024.

organization" that tries to provide important human services for the Palestinians whom they believe to be menaced by the massive Israeli war machine.

COLUMBIA UNIVERSITY: SJP AND JVP COME OUT FOR HAMAS

The increasingly hostile and even physically dangerous environment for Jews on many college and university campuses was largely the handiwork of the SJP and JVP. On October 9, 2023, when the full magnitude and horror of the October 7 invasion was just beginning to dawn on the world, the SJP and JVP chapters at Columbia University issued a full-throated declaration of support for Hamas, cloaked, of course, as support for the Palestinian "resistance." In light of what was already known about the massacre of some 1,200 Israelis, the statement is nothing short of grotesque. Signed by Columbia Students for Justice in Palestine and co-signed by Columbia Jewish Voice for Peace, it began:

> Columbia Students for Justice in Palestine stands in full solidarity with Palestinian resistance against over 75 years of Israeli settler-colonialism and apartheid. Palestinians have been subjected to the longest ongoing military occupation in modern history and their right to resist is enshrined in international law.[289]

Columbia's SJP unapologetically applauded the massacre, stating enthusiastically:

[289] Columbia SJP 10/9 Open Letter, October 9, 2023, https://docs.google.com/document/d/1RcXX5DEO3yfJ9R4ksURnzpIPCyVxo575-Y-SoC_vZFk/edit. Accessed October 30, 2024.

> Yesterday was an unprecedented historic moment for the Palestinians of Gaza, who tore through the wall that has been suffocating them in one of the most densely-populated areas on Earth for the past 16 years—an open-air prison blockaded by Israeli soldiers via land, air, and sea. Despite the odds against them, Palestinians launched a counter-offensive against their settler-colonial oppressor—which receives billions of US dollars annually in military aid and possesses one of the world's most robust surveillance and security apparatuses. Any omission of this context—any rhetoric of "an unprovoked Palestinian attack"—is shamefully misleading. We invite you to look into the detailed Human Rights Watch, B'tselem, and Amnesty International reports on Israeli apartheid.[290]

The SJP chapter came out unequivocally for jihad war against Israel:

> To those who are now calling for peace, we ask: where were you during the Great March of Return in 2018, when Palestinians in Gaza peacefully protested and were shot dead by the hundreds? Where were you when Israel indiscriminately bombed Palestinian civilians in Gaza in 2008, 2012, 2014, 2021, and 2022? Where were you this year, when Israel killed over 220 Palestinians over the past nine months alone?

[290] Ibid.

> Where were you as settlers kicked people out of their homes, arbitrarily imprisoned children without trial, and brutally oppressed an entire population?
>
> You are not asking for peace. You are asking for quiet submission to systemic violence.
>
> As long as you perpetuate this narrative, fighting will continue to break out until justice is achieved. Because nothing else is working.[291]

The statement added: "*We wholeheartedly condemn* the email sent by General Studies Dean Lisa Rosen-Metsch on October 8th that exclusively sympathized with Israeli soldiers who uphold the occupation, obfuscated Palestinian resistance against the Israeli military as 'terrorism,' and refused to acknowledge any of the hundreds of Palestinian casualties in the past 48 hours—let alone the overall context of the past 75 years. *We condemn* the October 7th email from Barnard Dean Leslie Grinage that extended support to those 'affected by the violence and loss of life in Israel' without even mentioning Palestinian suffering once."[292]

GETTING BANNED

As far left as Columbia University was, all this was too much. New York's WABC reported in mid-November 2023 that "Students for Justice in Palestine and Jewish Voice for Peace were suspended for the remainder of the fall semester after the university determined their protests for a cease-fire violated school policy.... Both of

[291] Ibid.
[292] Ibid.

the student groups have been critical of Israel amid the ongoing war with Hamas in the Middle East. University officials said they organized an unauthorized event and their rhetoric was 'threatening and intimidating' to certain constituencies on campus."[293]

Behaving in a threatening and intimidating manner toward those whom it hates seems to be the fundamental modus operandi of both groups.

The bans were enormously unpopular on the Columbia campus. WABC reported that on November 15, 2023, "hundreds of demonstrators took to the streets" in order to demonstrate their "support for the Palestinians in Gaza while demanding an end to campus censorship at Columbia University. Outside Columbia's administration building, 250 professors walked-out in protest, joining students and alumni—all furious over the university's decision to suspend the on-campus activities of two groups, critical of Israel: Students for Justice in Palestine and Jewish Voice for Peace."[294]

Several days later, there was another demonstration. The *Columbia Spectator* reported that "roughly 200 alumni organized a demonstration on Monday outside the gates at 116th Street and Amsterdam Avenue in protest of the University's suspension of its chapters of Students for Justice in Palestine and Jewish Voice for Peace. The protest was organized by CUAlumni4Palestine, a coalition group of alumni and affiliates of the University that

---

293 "Hundreds protest at Columbia over school's decision to suspend student groups calling for cease-fire," WABC, November 15, 2023, https://abc7ny.com/columbia-university-protests-israel-palestine/14064751/. Accessed October 30, 2024.

294 Ibid.

formed in the wake of the University's Nov. 10 announcement to suspend SJP and JVP."[295]

The cause of the professors' ire was clear: these two groups enunciated what they had been teaching students for years. The alumni were demonstrating how effectively they had been indoctrinated.

The SJP has become so shrill and intimidating in "uplifting" its demands regarding the Palestinians and Israel that in late October 2023, CNN reported that the Anti-Defamation League (ADL) had "sent an open letter to more than 200 colleges and universities Wednesday, urging administrators to investigate campus chapters of Students for Justice in Palestine for allegedly supporting Hamas."[296]

Florida Governor Ron DeSantis was ahead of the ADL, ordering the State University System of Florida to shut down SJP chapters at Florida colleges and universities, as part of a crackdown on demonstrations that displayed "harmful support for terrorist groups."[297] The system's Chancellor Ray Rodriguez stated that the SJP supported terror in a manner that implied that this support was beyond dispute: "Based on the National SJP's support of terrorism, in consultation with Governor DeSantis, the student chapters must be deactivated."[298]

In a similar vein, according to a mid-November 2023 *New York Times* report, "The group has been banned or suspended by

---

295 John Towfighi and Saul Quintanar, "Alumni protest suspension of SJP and JVP," Columbia Spectator, November 21, 2023, https://www.columbiaspectator.com/news/2023/11/21/alumni-protest-suspension-of-sjp-and-jvp/. Accessed October 30, 2024.

296 Jordan Valinsky, "Anti-Defamation League accuses pro-Palestine student groups of siding with terrorism," CNN, October 27, 2023, https://www.cnn.com/2023/10/27/business/adl-open-letter-colleges-spj/index.html. Accessed October 30, 2024.

297 Andrew Hay, "Florida's DeSantis bans pro-Palestinian student group," Reuters, October 26, 2023, https://www.reuters.com/world/us/floridas-desantis-bans-pro-palestinian-student-group-2023-10-25/. Accessed October 30, 2024.

298 Ibid.

Brandeis, Columbia and George Washington University. And it was recently the target of thundering speeches on Capitol Hill and blistered during a Republican presidential debate."[299] Brandeis President Ron Liebowitz issued a statement on November 8, 2023, explaining: "Monday, the university issued a decision to no longer recognize the Brandeis chapter of the National Students for Justice in Palestine (SJP). This decision was made because SJP openly supports Hamas, which the United States has designated as a Foreign Terrorist Organization, and its call for the violent elimination of Israel and the Jewish people."[300]

At George Washington University, according to the *Washington Post*, "Students for Justice in Palestine (SJP) at GWU projected multiple images on the Estelle and Melvin Gelman Library on October 24, the GWU statement on Tuesday said. Jewish student groups among others have objected to the images, which were in the form of slogans, and described them as potentially antisemitic. One of the projections, according to photographs, was the phrase 'Divestment from Zionist genocide now.' Others included 'Glory to our martyrs' and the slogan 'Free Palestine from the river to the sea.'"[301]

"From the river to the sea" has unmistakable genocidal overtones; if Israel were destroyed altogether, from the Jordan River to the Mediterranean Sea, where would its seven million Jews go? In October 2015, a Hamas-linked Muslim cleric and

---

[299] Alan Blinder, "Inside the Pro-Palestinian Group Protesting Across College Campuses," New York Times, November 17, 2023, https://www.nytimes.com/2023/11/17/us/students-justice-palestine-campus-protests.html. Accessed October 30, 2024.

[300] Ron Liebowitz, "A space for free speech, not hate speech," Brandeis University, November 8, 2023. https://www.brandeis.edu/president/letters/2023-11-08-free-speech-not-hate-speech.html. Accessed October 30, 2024.

[301] Martin Weil and Susan Svrluga, "GWU suspends group over projection of pro-Palestinian slogans," Washington Post, November 15, 2023, https://www.brandeis.edu/president/letters/2023-11-08-free-speech-not-hate-speech.html. Accessed October 30, 2024.

TV personality, Sheikh Iyad Abu Funun, declared on Hamas' al-Aqsa television channel "that not a single Jew will remain on this land."[302] He added, "We will not leave a single one of you, alive or dead, on this land. By Allah, we will dig up your bones from your graves and get them out of this country."[303] Quite clearly, millions would be killed.

These bans led to calls for more. In late November 2023, the *New York Post* reported that "A bipartisan group of more than three dozen lawmakers" called on New York Governor Kathy Hochul to ban the SJP. They wrote: "For years, a major growing cause of concern on college campuses has been a group called 'Students for Justice in Palestine' (SJP), which has chapters throughout American Universities. At their events, SJP members and allies chant things like 'from New York to Gaza, Globalize the Intifada,' 'when people are occupied, resistance is justified,' and 'from the river to the sea, Palestine will be free.' These chants are from the Hamas charter and call for the death and annihilation of Jews and Israel."[304]

At Columbia, however, the ban did little good. No sooner was the SJP banned that it rebranded itself as Columbia Social Workers 4 Palestine, a group that appeared only in the wake of the controversy over the SJP's statement and the banning of the group. On November 29, 2023, it held a "Teach-In" on

---

302 "Hamas Cleric and TV Host Abu Funun: We Will Not Leave a Single Jew, Dead or Alive, on Our Land," MEMRI, October 13, 2015, https://www.memri.org/tv/hamas-cleric-and-tv-host-abu-funun-we-will-not-leave-single-jew-dead-or-alive-our-land. Accessed October 30, 2024.

303 Ibid.

304 Craig McCarthy, "Bipartisan group of lawmakers call for ban of pro-Hamas student group in NY," New York Post, November 20, 2023, https://www.msn.com/en-us/news/us/bipartisan-group-of-lawmakers-call-for-ban-of-pro-hamas-student-group-in-ny/ar-AA1kfyT5. Accessed October 30, 2024.

"Palestine and Imperialism."[305] Its announcement of the event on X featured an outline of the discussion, which began with a long quote from Lenin and then followed with a heavily Marxism-influenced "History of Zionism."[306] It declared that "'peace negotiations' on the question of Palestine have always served U.S. imperialists' monopolization of the Middle East."

Then on December 3, 2023, Columbia Social Workers 4 Palestine announced on X that it was hosting an event entitled: "Significance of the October 7th Palestinian Counteroffensive."[307] The group explained, "We will discuss the significance of the Palestinian counteroffensive on October 7th and the centrality of revolutionary violence to anti-imperialism. See y'all there!"[308] Again justifying Palestinian jihad violence against Israeli civilians, the group added, "In advocating for Palestinian liberation, Palestinians have engaged in nonviolent resistance tactics for years. These peaceful actions have been met with tear gas and armed opposition by the Israeli government."[309]

Whatever the exact relationship may be between Columbia Social Workers 4 Palestine and the campus SJP chapter, there is little doubt that SJP members would approve of this rhetoric, which so closely recalled the SJP's own statement in the wake of the October 7 massacre.

---

305 "Columbia School of Social Work student group to host pro-Oct 7 'teach-in,'" Jerusalem Post, December 4, 2023, https://www.jpost.com/international/article-776466. Accessed October 30, 2024.

306 Ibid.

307 Daksha Pillai and Sabrina Ticer-Wurr, "School of Social Work students hold 'Palestinian Counteroffensive' teach-in despite cancellation by administration," by Columbia Daily Spectator, December 8, 2023. https://www.columbiaspectator.com/news/2023/12/08/school-of-social-work-students-hold-palestinian-counteroffensive-teach-in-despite-cancellation-by-administration/. Accessed October 30, 2024.

308 Ibid.

309 "Columbia School of Social Work student group," op. cit.

CHAPTER FOURTEEN

JEWISH VOICES FOR JIHAD

JEWISH COMRADES-IN-ARMS

The SJP's Jewish partner in Jew-hatred, Jewish Voice for Peace, is forthright about its leftism: "We envision a world," its website proclaims, "where all people—from the U.S. to Palestine—live in freedom, justice, equality, and dignity. Like generations of Jewish leftists before us, we fight for the liberation of all people. We believe that through organizing, we can and will dismantle the institutions and structures that sustain injustice and grow something new, joyful, beautiful, and life-sustaining in their place."[310]

JVP amplifies this claim to fight for the liberation of all with a millennial vision of a paradisal world, free from all conflict: "We picture the concrete of the Apartheid wall in pieces on free Palestinian soil. We picture Israeli jails, prisons, and detention centers emptied and dismantled. We picture the

310 "About," Jewish Voice for Peace, https://www.jewishvoiceforpeace.org/about/. Accessed October 30, 2024.

return of Palestinian refugees, reuniting with their families and communities. We picture Palestinians—from the Jordan River to the Mediterranean Sea—living with their inalienable rights respected, building schools and hospitals and planting olive groves with the resources they need."[311]

This will involve the liberation of Israelis as well, from their role as oppressors of the Palestinians: "We imagine Jewish Israelis released from conscripted violence against Palestinians, free from dehumanizing others which in turn diminishes their own humanity. We imagine Jewish Israelis joining Palestinians to build a just society, rooted in equality rather than supremacy, dignity rather than domination, democracy rather than dispossession—a society where every life is precious."[312]

It is clear from all this irenic fantasy that JVP assumes the Israeli/Palestinian conflict to be entirely the fault and responsibility of the Israelis. If only the Israelis didn't engage in apartheid, jail Palestinians, and prevent the return of Palestinians refugees! If only Israel didn't force its citizens to make war on the Palestinians, and dehumanize them, rather than join them in building a just society! The JVP says nothing about picturing the Palestinians ending the genocidal rhetoric against Jews that blankets their media, even for the youngest children. It doesn't picture the Palestinians recognizing the Jewish state's right to exist. It doesn't call upon them to close the jihad summer camps, or to stop preaching jihad as the highest virtue and the destruction of Israel as every Palestinians' goal. The Palestinians, in the JVP's view, are wholly innocent and unthreatening. If only the Israelis weren't so intransigent, peace would dawn in the region.

---

311 "Our Vision," Jewish Voice for Peace, https://www.jewishvoiceforpeace.org/resource/our-vision/. Accessed October 30, 2024.

312 Ibid.

Can the JVP really be this naïve? Some among its rank and file no doubt are. It is likely, however, that the leadership, with its rhetoric of "equality rather than supremacy, dignity rather than domination, democracy rather than dispossession," is attempting to appeal to the well-intentioned, uninformed and misinformed, while turning a blind eye to Palestinian hatred, incitement and violence in pursuit of the common Marxist/Islamic goal of the destruction of Israel. Internationalists hate the Jewish state for perpetuating the idea of individual ethnicities forming nation-states; Muslims hate it for being a state ruled by the worst enemies of the Muslims, the Jews (cf. Qur'an 5:82), on land they believe belongs to Islam. That message, however, wouldn't play nearly as well to the low-information public as talk of equality, dignity, and democracy.

JVP was founded in 1996 by four University of California students, Julia Caplan, Raichel Eisner, Julie Iny, and Mitchell Plitnick. A founding member was the staunchly anti-Israel Stanford professor Joel Beinin. As of this writing, it has fifty-seven chapters on college and university campuses all over the country.[313] It states its goals in Jewish terms, with the goal of driving a wedge between Judaism and Zionism: "While our mission is to build and mobilize enough power to change Olam HaZeh, the world as it is, we also seek to embody Ha'Olam She'Ba—the world to come—right here and now. When you organize with us, you are part of building a Jewishness and Jewish life beyond Zionism."[314] Heike Schotten of the JVP chapter in Boston added that the JVP was intended to "drive a wedge between Zionism

313 "Interested in joining a JVP chapter or pod?," https://www.jewishvoiceforpeace.org/local/#section-Chapters. Accessed October 30, 2024.

314 "Our Vision," Jewish Voice for Peace, https://mobile.x.com/VarietyPack2/status/1842097475051467235. Accessed October 30, 2024.

and Judaism, demonstrating by their very existence that not all Jews are Zionists."[315]

JVP Executive Director Rebecca Vilkomerson has also identified JVP as a movement of solidarity with the Palestinian jihad: "I think part of our job as the Jewish wing of the [Palestinian solidarity] movement, is to facilitate conversations inside the Jewish community.... So, I think it's very important to think sort of how we plan a wedge.... So, I think that the more and more we can sort of put that wedge in, saying the Jewish community's not agreeing on these issues, the more we'll make progress."[316]

Accordingly, the JVP sees no problem allying with the pro-Hamas Students for Justice In Palestine. In fact, while attributing the rise in antisemitism to Israel's alleged misdeeds, it has a project entitled "The Network Against Islamophobia (NAI)," which "provides support and resources for those interested in organizing against Islamophobia and anti-Arab racism."[317] This network was "created to serve as a resource to, and work with, JVP chapters and other Jewish groups and to be a partner to the broader, Muslim-led movement against Islamophobia."[318] It seeks "to build connections among Jewish Voice for Peace chapters and other groups working on these issues to effectively challenge Islamophobia in our local communities and develop our thinking together."[319]

As is characteristic of leftists, JVP sees Islamic jihad attacks only as a pretext for the "Islamophobia" that they present as a

---

315 Rachel Avraham, "The 'Jewish Voice For Peace' is Anti-Israel & Anti-Peace," United With Israel, August 4, 2013, https://www.jewishpress.com/blogs/united-with-israel/the-jewish-voice-for-peace-is-anti-israel-anti-peace/2013/08/06/. Accessed October 30, 2024.

316 Ibid.

317 "About the Network Against Islamophobia," Jewish Voice for Peace, https://www.jewishvoiceforpeace.org/2015/12/03/refugees-welcome/. Accessed October 30, 2024.

318 Ibid.

319 Ibid.

far greater problem. In January 2015, when Islamic jihadis murdered twelve people at the offices of the satirical *Charlie Hebdo* magazine in Paris for the crime of lampooning the Islamic prophet Muhammad, JVP's Network Against Islamophobia issued a statement assuring the world that it mourned for "those killed in the murderous attacks in Paris this week at the offices of *Charlie Hebdo* magazine and in the kosher supermarket." Then, without bothering to condemn killings incited by Sharia blasphemy laws or utter any remotely critical word regarding Islam, the statement continued, "We also stand in strong opposition to increasing Islamophobia and racism in response to these murders—the vilifying of Muslims and attributing to all Muslims the acts of a few who claim to speak in the name of Islam."[320]

JVP claimed that "French Muslims especially are bearing the brunt of the current backlash," but the problem could be found elsewhere as well: "Muslims are at greatly heightened risk from the forces of bigotry. This latest backlash occurs in the context of pervasive, systemic, and long-standing anti-Islam bigotry in many countries around the world. In Germany, for example, even before the Paris shootings, mobs shouting anti-Muslim slogans marched through the streets. In the United States, an anti-Muslim, right-wing network of media outlets, politicians, and professional Islamophobes has predictably seized on the murders as fuel for its continued hate-filled speech and actions."[321]

---

320 "The Paris Murders & the Islamophobic Backlash," Jewish Voice for Peace, January 13, 2015, https://www.jewishvoiceforpeace.org/2015/01/13/the-paris-murders-the-islamophobic-backlash/. Accessed October 30, 2024.

321 Ibid.

WHERE THE MONEY COMES FROM

In April 2016, Jonathan Schanzer of the Foundation for the Defense of Democracies testified before a joint hearing of the House Foreign Affairs Committee's Subcommittee on Terrorism, Nonproliferation, and Trade and the Subcommittee on the Middle East and North Africa that the chief source of funding for SJP chapters was Hatem Bazian's other organization, American Muslims for Palestine. Schanzer stated that "AMP is arguably the most important sponsor and organizer for Students for Justice in Palestine (SJP), which is the most visible arm of the BDS campaign on campuses in the United States. AMP provides speakers, training, printed materials, a so-called 'Apartheid Wall,' and grants to SJP activists. AMP even has a campus coordinator on staff whose job is to work directly with SJP and other pro-BDS campus groups across the country. According to an email it sent to subscribers, AMP spent $100,000 on campus activities in 2014 alone."[322]

The JVP appears to have garnered more support from the mainstream left, although NGO Monitor noted in May 2016 that JVP "is not transparent about funding sources."[323] However, it enjoys generous funding: "Limited financial information on JVP is available through public IRS documents (990s) and databases, which report a total budget of $1,407,148 for 2014."[324] In its own investigation, for the years 2014 and 2015, NGO

[322] Jonathan Schanzer, "Israel Imperiled: Threats to the Jewish State," Foundation for the Defense of Democracies, April 19, 2016, https://docs.house.gov/meetings/FA/FA18/20160419/104817/HHRG-114-FA18-Wstate-SchanzerJ-20160419.pdf. Accessed October 30, 2024.

[323] "Uncovering the Jewish Voice for Peace (JVP) Funding Network," NGO Monitor, May 1, 2016, https://ngo-monitor.org/reports/uncovering-the-jvp-funding-network/. Accessed October 30, 2024.

[324] Ibid.

Monitor "was able to identify $626,793 in donations and grants awarded to JVP. Our research reveals that JVP received funding from a broad range of foundations and charitable trusts, many of which, unsurprisingly, also contribute to other anti-Israel organizations."[325] These groups include "Rockefeller Brothers Fund ($140,000 in 2015); Tides Foundation ($49,477 in 2014); Firedoll Foundation ($25,000 in 2014); Schwab Charitable Foundation ($158,800 in 2014); Jewish Communal Fund (S25,100 in 2015)."[326] It is likely, however, that the donations from Schwab and the Jewish Communal Fund were made on behalf of others who wished to remain anonymous. Nonetheless, it was clear that JVP enjoyed widespread support among Jewish leftists, and likely also among many Jews who were not familiar with its opposition to Israel and alliance with jihad forces, and who assumed that it was a benign organization.

THE GRADUATES

"The evil that men do lives after them," says Mark Antony in Shakespeare's *Julius Caesar*, and the same can be said of SJP and JVP. Although students only stay in college for a few years, often the beliefs and attitudes that are formed there remain with them for their entire lifetime. In the aftermath of the October 7 massacre, there were demonstrations against Israel not only on campuses, but in cities all across the country. Filling the ranks of many of these demonstrations, which included tens of thousands of people, were current and former members of campus chapters of Students for Justice in Palestine and Jewish Voice for Peace.

325 Ibid.
326 Ibid.

The prime mover behind these demonstrations, however, was a group known as the People's Forum, which, like the JVP, speaks about its mission in strongly Marxist language. "We are a movement incubator," it says on its website, "for working class and marginalized communities to build unity across historic lines of division at home and abroad. We are an accessible educational and cultural space that nurtures the next generation of visionaries and organizers who believe that through collective action a new world is possible."[327]

The primary funding for the People's Forum comes from a multimillionaire Marxist software entrepreneur, Neville Roy Singham, along with his wife, Jodie Evans, a co-founder of the far-left activist group Code Pink, which shares the JVP's view of Israel. According to a November 2023 *Free Press* exposé, "Last month, a group of Code Pink followers disrupted a Senate Appropriations Committee to chant for a cease-fire in Israel as they held up their red-painted hands—calling to mind a famous 2000 image of a Palestinian man who waved his blood-soaked hands to celebrate the lynching of two IDF reservists."[328]

Free Press adds that "a review of public disclosure forms show that multimillionaire Singham and his wife Evans have donated over $20.4 million to The People's Forum from 2017 to 2022 through a series of shell organizations and donor advisory groups—accounting for nearly all of the group's funding."[329] Wherever its money comes from, the People's Forum is quite

---

[327] "About," The People's Forum, https://peoplesforum.org/about/. Accessed October 30, 2024.

[328] Francesca Block, "The American Multimillionaire Marxists Funding Pro-Palestinian Rage," The Free Press, November 14, 2023, https://www.thefp.com/p/american-marxists-funding-pro-palestinian-rage. Accessed October 30, 2024.

[329] Ibid.

wealthy: "As of 2021, the organization employed 13 staff members and held more than $13.6 million in total assets."[330]

Singham, meanwhile, is much more than just a Marxist millionaire who hates Israel. "He is also a China sympathizer who lives in Shanghai and has close ties to at least four propaganda news sites that boost the Chinese Communist Party's image abroad." In 2008, he was quoted in a Fortune magazine profile: "China is teaching the West that the world is better off with a dual system of both free-market adjustments and long-term planning."[331] Singham and Evans now live in Shanghai.

The People's Forum is openly Marxist. "At its multiroom modern headquarters in Midtown, which anyone can visit, The People's Forum hosts classes like 'Lenin and the Path to Revolution,' praising countries like China and Cuba that have 'smash[ed] the shackles of Western imperialism,' as well as seminars like 'Healthcare Under Siege and Apartheid,' blaming Israel for 'discriminatory policies' and 'genocide' in Gaza. Its bookshop, 1804 Books—named after the year Haiti overthrew its French rulers—is stocked with hundreds of titles celebrating Communist heroes from Karl Marx to Che Guevara."[332]

Like so many Marxist entities, the People's Forum is popular among corporate leftists: "According to tax filings from 2018 to 2021, the forum spent over $12 million in 'leasehold improvements' to their office space. Reviewing publicly available documents, *The Free Press* traced the money from Singham to The People's Forum via a fund run by Goldman Sachs, which operates a philanthropy arm that enables wealthy clients to give

---

330 Ibid.

331 David Kirkpatrick, "The socialist state of ThoughtWorks," Fortune, March 17, 2008, https://money.cnn.com/2008/03/14/technology/kirkpatrick_thoughtworks.fortune/index.htm. Accessed October 30, 2024.

332 Block, "The American Multimillionaire Marxists," op. cit.

large donations to nonprofit causes. The fund, which operates separately from the bank, also serves to help donors conceal their identities."

At the moment, the People's Forum's Marxist agitprop is directed at destroying the Jewish state. "For now, the People's Forum is focusing on its pro-Palestinian agenda, calling for 'more marches, walk-outs, sit-ins, and other forms of direct action directed at the political offices, businesses, and workplaces that fund, invest, and collaborate with Israeli genocide and occupation.'"[333] Manolo De Los Santos, executive director of the People's Forum, excoriated a post-October 7 pro-Israel march in Washington as a "Pro-Genocide March," smearing its guest speakers as "racists" and "fake progressives."[334] Meanwhile, regarding the November 4 Free Palestine rally in Washington, which the People's Forum co-organized, De Los Santos said proudly, "We didn't bow down to demands to be respectable."

Indeed. There is nothing respectable about the Marxist/Islamic imperative, on campus and off, to destroy the state of Israel and deny the Jewish people, out of all the peoples of the world, the right of self-determination. The greatest contribution that the People's Forum makes to that imperative is not a financial one, or its organizational acumen. The greatest contribution that the People's Forum makes to the anti-Israel movement is making its Marxist roots and goals clear and undeniable.

Together, Students for Justice in Palestine, Jewish Voice for Peace, and the People's Forum form a sinister triumvirate that together makes for a solid front against Israel. On campuses, young and impressionable Muslim and non-Muslim students

---

333 Ibid.

334 Ibid.

are recruited into anti-Israel activism by being convinced that Israel is an oppressive apartheid state that systematically violates the human rights of Palestinians. Then these groups provide an abundant outlet for the anger they have created, and give the student the sense of being part of a great and noble cause. Once the student graduates, the People's Forum allows him or her to continue his activism in this supposedly righteous cause.

The convergence of the left and the forces of Islam on the issue of Israel and the Palestinians was quite similar in form and intent to the fabrication of Islam's fictional historical achievements. Both were designed to exalt what was at its core a struggle for domination and the subjugation of non-Muslims, to render that struggle noble, and to celebrate it as just. The fantasists about Islamic history ennobled the historical jihad, while leftist political activists did the same favor for the most famous jihad of the present day. No one involved in either endeavor took the trouble to notice what Islam actually taught about unbelievers, or what its ideal society had in store for them.

CHAPTER FIFTEEN

FABRICATED MUSLIMS

STEALING GENIUSES

With Islam's fabricated past and fabricated present-day struggle for justice come fabricated Muslims. Modern-day Islamic apologists frequently claim that some eminent figure of great accomplishment was actually a Muslim, usually a secret or deathbed convert. Once again, the inferiority complex is clear. There are not enough people of great accomplishment in the Islamic world, so they have to be borrowed from elsewhere.

In 2012, the grandson of a prominent Iranian cleric, the Ayatollah Hossein Borujerdi, made a startling claim: Albert Einstein, he asserted, was "corresponding with the cleric and had admitted Shia Islam was the most scientific and just religion in the world."[335] The grandson further claimed that letters that Borujerdi and Einstein exchanged that would establish Einstein's

---

[335] "Iranian cleric: Albert Einstein was Shiite Muslim," Haaretz, March 8, 2014, https://www.haaretz.com/2014-03-08/ty-article/iranian-cleric-einstein-was-shiite/0000017f-f824-d2d5-a9ff-f8acedaf0000. Accessed October 30, 2024.

conversion to Shi'ite Islam were preserved in a secure location in London.

Two years later, another Iranian Muslim cleric, Ayatollah Mahadavi Kani, the head of the Islamic Republic of Iran's Assembly of Experts, the body that chooses the Supreme Leader, also stated that Albert Einstein was, in fact, a Shi'ite Muslim. Kani claimed that Einstein's conversion was thoroughly documented, and that it came about because of his scientific investigations.

According to Kani, Einstein recounted that when he heard about Muhammad's journey to paradise, during which he conversed with his fellow prophets and met Allah himself, the great thinker realized that what was being described was "a process which was faster than the speed of light."[336] Einstein realized, said Kani, that "this is the very same relativity movement" that he had been studying.[337] Kani added: "Einstein said, 'when I heard about the narratives of the prophet Muhammad and that of the Ahle-Beit [Muhammad's household] I realized they had understood these things way before us."[338]

What can be done with this? Even to look into the details of Einstein's biography in order to find disconfirming evidence regarding this claim would be to take it far too seriously. Yet Borujerdi and Kani were completely serious, and in their earnestness only managed to call attention to Islam's deep inferiority complex. Having no Einstein of their own, just as they appropriate the sacred sites of conquered people (such as the Temple Mount and the Hagia Sophia cathedral in Constantinople) in order to assert the superiority and supremacy of Islam, so also

336 Ibid.
337 Ibid.
338 Ibid.

they claim the great minds of the Western world and dress them in Islamic clothing.

Yet while a building can be appropriated, or demolished and built over, a person is not so easily appropriated. Nonetheless, the stealing of Einstein was not singular. Two years before Einstein's conversion was announced to the world, the Islamic Republic of Iran's state-controlled Ahlul Bayt News Agency ran a feature about a new book, *Leonardo Da Vinci's Drawings*, by the Iranian writer Morteza Khalaj Amirhosseini. "I have prepared the book," Amirhosseini explained, "in order to address the needs of art students as there was no comprehensive book of Da Vinci's works available in Iran. We should know an artist by his works, but unfortunately Da Vinci is just an icon in Iran with mythological fame."[339]

That was all very well, but Amirhosseini then demonstrated that he was just as much given to flights of fancy as the Westerners who eagerly supported the 1001 Inventions exhibits, and "went on to say that the book presents a complete biography of Da Vinci in which he has proved based on first-hand sources that the Renaissance artist had become a Muslim. However, the west prefers to keep silent on the subject, he added."[340] Amirhosseini asserted that "a French writer in the nineteenth century has evaluated the issue of Da Vinci's conversion to Islam in a treatise, but the west has banned the publication of this treatise."[341]

That was where Amirhosseini's claims really strained credulity. The West of the likes of Diana Darke and Jim Knight would not have banned the publication of evidence that Da Vinci was

339 "Da Vinci was a Muslim?," Ahlul Bayt News Agency, April 9, 2012, https://en.abna24.com/story/307415. Accessed October 30, 2024.

340 Ibid.

341 Ibid.

a Muslim. Such news would have been trumpeted far and wide, if it had really existed, and would have been hailed everywhere as yet more evidence of the tolerant, peaceful, enlightened Islam that everyone in the West was confident was the true manifestation of the religion, which would appear any minute now. In June 2011, the US Ambassador to Qatar, Joseph LeBaron, made an optimistic prediction, "Let me give you a 30-year perspective. Since I first came to the Gulf in 1980, I have seen the Gulf states pursue a pattern of growth that is leading, whether consciously or unconsciously, towards a highly ambitious goal: a renaissance of Arab and Islamic thought in science and technology. It's extraordinary, actually. The amazing thing is that both the resources and, increasingly, the vision are there to accomplish this renaissance."[342]

We're still waiting.

THE CALL TO PRAYER ON THE MOON

One of the most popular and persistent of these exercises in wishful thinking is the claim that Neil Armstrong, the first man on the moon, converted to Islam as a result of his lunar experience. In October 2018, the *Washington Post* saw fit to address and refute this claim; the *Post* writer recounted that in Indonesia she encountered a man who "told me, matter of factly, that when Armstrong was visiting the Middle East several years after his Apollo flight, he heard the call of the muezzin and asked what it was. Upon being informed of the sound's source, the story went,

342 "U.S. Ambassador Joseph LeBaron: 'The Arab Spring is the Start of a Long, Uncertain Path to Structural Change in the Middle East,'" Knowledge At Wharton, June 28, 2011, https://knowledge.wharton.upenn.edu/article/u-s-ambassador-joseph-lebaron-the-arab-spring-is-the-start-of-a-long-uncertain-path-to-structural-change-in-the-middle-east/. Accessed October 30, 2024.

Armstrong said he had heard the very same sound on the moon. In the legend, he converted to Islam on the spot."[343]

Armstrong even responded to this claim himself: "I have found that many organizations claim me as a member, for which I am not a member, and a lot of different families—Armstrong families and others—make connections, many of which don't exist. So many people identify with the success of Apollo. The claim about my becoming a Muslim is just an extreme version of people inevitably telling me they know somebody whom I might know."[344] Nevertheless, "over the years, Armstrong was inundated by requests to appear at Islamic religious observances around the world. He was so deluged that he worked with the State Department in 1983 to send a rejection of the claim to embassies and consulates throughout the Middle East, North Africa and Asia. It states: 'While stressing his strong desire not to offend anyone or show disrespect for any religion, Armstrong has advised Department that reports of his conversion to Islam are inaccurate.... If Post receives queries on this matter, Armstrong requests that they politely but firmly inform querying party that he has not converted to Islam and has no current plans or desire to travel overseas to participate in Islamic religious activities.'"[345]

THE UNDERSEA WORLD OF ISLAM

"In France," *Arab News* reported excitedly in September 2013, "Islam is very quickly spreading among those people, who have

343 Sally Tyler, "The false, but persistent, rumor that Neil Armstrong converted to Islam," Washington Post, October 12, 2018, https://www.washingtonpost.com/outlook/2018/10/12/false-persistent-rumor-that-neil-armstrong-converted-islam/. Accessed October 30, 2024.

344 Ibid.

345 Ibid.

become famous in the most different fields of knowledge and activity. Today, the number of people, who left Christianity and accepted Islam has already reached over a hundred thousand. Archbishop Parisian, the supreme ecclesiastic of the French Catholic church, officially confirms these figures."[346]

There was, of course, no such person as "Archbishop Parisian." That was not *Arab News*' only flight of fancy. It went on to make this claim: "Great French scientist, oceanographer, initiator of researches of sea and ocean depths, inventor of an aqualung, underwater house, the device for 'diving saucer,' author of many popular books and films, Jacque IV [sic] Cousteau is known all through the world. But very few people know, that scientific researches carried out by him and facts of reflection in the Qur'an of many scientific signs have led him to accept Islam; and that he died as a Muslim."[347]

Cousteau "declared that choice of embracing Islam was most correct decision in his life."[348] Like Armstrong, he supposedly converted due to the experience of a natural phenomenon: "In 1962," *Arab News* quotes Cousteau as saying, "German scientists found out that in Bab Al-Mandeb, where waters of Gulf of Aden and Red sea converge, waters of Red sea and Indian ocean do not mix up."[349]

Cousteau later "found out that this is already written in Qur'an for more than 1400 years back. He learned about it from the French doctor Maurice Bucaille, who had earlier accepted Islam. 'When I told to him about my discovery, he told me that this has already been told 1400 years back in Qur'an. It was for me

346 "How Jacques Cousteau accepted Islam," Arab News, September 13, 2013.
347 Ibid.
348 Ibid.
349 Ibid.

as thundering during clear sky. And it really so appeared when I looked at translations of Qur'an. Then I exclaimed: "I swear, that this Qur'an, which 1400 years ago lagged behind modern science, cannot be the speech of a person. It is true speech of Almighty." After that I accepted Islam and each day I was amazed by truth, justice, ease, utility of this religion. I am indefinitely grateful that He opened my eyes for Truth."[350]

A charming story, but a fictional one. When Cousteau died in 1997, he was given a Roman Catholic funeral. The Cousteau Foundation has denied claims that he converted to Islam.

NON-MUSLIMS MAKING MUSLIMS

This game was so much fun, at least one non-Muslim Westerner couldn't resist joining in: none other than Thomas Jefferson, the author of the Declaration of Independence and third president of the United States.

Jefferson famously wrote that "neither pagan nor Mahamedan nor Jew ought to be excluded from the civil rights of the Commonwealth because of his religion."[351] During the acrimonious 1800 presidential campaign, the *Connecticut Courant* warned that it was impossible to ascertain "whether Mr. Jefferson believes in the heathen mythology or in the alcoran [Qur'an]; whether he is a Jew or a Christian; whether he believes in one God, or in many; or in none at all."[352]

This was fairly standard campaign rhetoric for the time, but contemporary historian Denise Spellberg saw much more in it

350 Ibid.

351 David Tormsen, "10 Conspiracy Theories About Famous People Converting To Islam," ListVerse, January 31, 2016, https://listverse.com/2016/01/31/10-conspiracy-theories-about-famous-people-converting-to-islam/. Accessed October 11, 2024.

352 Ibid.

than that. In her eyes, this charge conferred upon Jefferson a particular honor: being accused of being a Muslim. "For centuries," she wrote, "it had been common in Europe for one Christian to defame another with references to Islam, a practice that crossed the Atlantic. Jefferson, for his expansive views of religious liberty and political equality, would be attacked repeatedly as an 'infidel,' a word that in his time meant not just an 'unbeliever,' but a Muslim."[353]

This was not precisely true. The *Courant* was simply saying that Jefferson's beliefs were unclear, and that his believing in the Qur'an was one possibility. In Spellberg's anxiousness to demonstrate that "Islamophobia" had always been part of the American experience, she omitted the other possibilities that the *Courant* mentioned. Spellberg added that "Jefferson owned a Quran," which she took to be an indication that he admired Islam; the idea that he might have had the book in order to understand the mindset of the Barbary pirates who went to war with the United States during his administration is left unexamined.

THE MUSLIM MORGAN FREEMAN

On November 22, 2022, the Facebook page All Sports posted a photo of the famed actor Morgan Freeman with this caption in Arabic: "The biggest news of the day..!! Famous Hollywood actor Morgan Freeman converted to Islam. May Allah Almighty make us steadfast in Islam. Amen." The post concluded with the hashtags "#FIFAWorldCup" and "#FIFAWorldCupQatar2022,"

353 Denise A. Spellberg, "Jefferson Was the First President Defamed for Mentioning Islam," Muslim Village, January 14, 2014, https://www.cairoklahoma.com/blog/jefferson-was-the-first-president-defamed-for-mentioning-islam/. Accessed October 30, 2024.

implying that Freeman had embraced Islam while in Qatar for the World Cup.[354]

A variant of the story added this claim: "Form [sic] Denmark newspaper: Morgan Freeman: In fact, the Arab culture of #Qatar made me love Islam more and I will spread what happened to me among my friends and family about love, respect and human appreciation among Muslims here. God gave me a vision of the right path, and Doha presented the world with the most beautiful in history."[355]

As it turned out, this was all fantasy. A fact-checking site, Soch Fact Check "browsed articles related to the 2022 FIFA World Cup but did not find any credible reports suggesting that Morgan Freeman has converted to Islam."[356] Corrections went out worldwide: "International Fact-Checking Network (IFCN) signatory *Reuters* quoted Freeman representative Fred Specktor as saying, 'Morgan has not converted to Islam.' *Misbar*—an Arabic fact-checking outlet—has also debunked the claim."[357]

Soch Fact Check even checked for the "Denmark newspaper" that had reported on Freeman's alleged enthusiasm for Islam and came up empty, finding "no credible report carrying the 'God gave me a vision of the right path' quote being attributed to the eighty-five-year-old actor. We also searched Google using

354 All Sports, caption in Arabic, Facebook, November 22, 2022, https://www.facebook.com/permalink.php?story_fbid=pfbid02dL3aE96M5M2ATkijZLzm3AknuHss-Mc6N1BTkkcKUhrkBQDR1XkMiSc7n36sGQnDDl&id=100078464799070. Accessed October 22, 2024.

355 Haseem uz Zaman, "False claim Morgan Freeman has converted to Islam goes viral," Soch Fact Check, December 1, 2022, https://www.sochfactcheck.com/morgan-freeman-converted-to-islam-false-claim-goes-viral-2022-fifa-world-cup-qatar/. Accessed October 22, 2024.

356 Ibid.

357 Ibid.

portions of the quote translated into Danish, considering the posts claim it is from a Denmark newspaper."[358]

Why imagine that Morgan Freeman had converted to Islam? After all, quite a few celebrities actually had converted to Islam, including boxer Cassius Clay (Muhammad Ali), basketball star Lew Alcindor (Kareem Abdul-Jabbar), and singer Cat Stevens (Yusuf Islam). Why was there so much insecurity among at least some Muslims that new converts had to be invented, and even, in at least one case, an entire eminent person who converted to Islam was fabricated out of whole cloth?

THE MUSLIM JOHN FORD

Even fictional notables convert to Islam. In December 2021, some Muslims were abuzz with the claim that a certain "John Ford" had converted to Islam. The John Ford in question was not the famed film director who gave the world *Stagecoach* and *The Man Who Shot Liberty Valance*—that John Ford died in 1973. Rather, the claim was that America's wealthiest man had found faith in Allah: "ALLAHU AKBAR. John Ford, the richest man in America, owns 190 American channels. He declared his conversion to Islam and cried while pronouncing the shadah," that is, the shahadah, the Islamic profession of faith.[359] "May Allah bless him Ameen."[360]

The post was accompanied by two photos of a respectable-looking white-haired gentleman in a gray suit, clearly overcome by some powerful emotion.

---

358 Ibid.

359 Abishek Mandadi, "The claim that John Ford, the richest man in America had converted to Islam is false," Factly, January 4, 2022, https://factly.in/the-claim-that-john-ford-the-richest-man-in-america-had-converted-to-islam-is-false/. Accessed October 22, 2024.

360 Ibid.

Reactions from Muslims on Facebook were jubilant: "allahu akber masha allah welcome the true religion"; "Mashaa Allah, welcome to the universe of ISLAM, PEACE, The true religion"; "Masha Allah. Thanks Allah swt for giving u chance to become people of JANNAH..MAY ALLAH SWT CONTINUE TO GUIDE U ALWAYS,..." and the like.[361] "Allahu akbar" means "Allah is greater," that is, greater than all other gods. "Masha Allah" means "Allah has willed it." "SWT" stands for "subhanahu wa ta'ala," that is, "Glory be to him, the exalted one." "Jannah" is paradise.

The joy over John Ford's conversion, however, was misplaced. The Indian fact-checking website Factly reported in January 2022 that the photos accompanying the article were not certainly those of a man named John Ford, and that the claims made about this Ford could not be verified. "The photo of the person is rumoured to be of a US Army leader who was saying the Shahada (prayer of initiation into the faith) in a video that had gone viral in 2018 in Oman. The name of the person could not be identified. There is no person named 'John Ford' in 'The 10 Richest People in America From 2010–2021' list given by Forbes. There are no recent news articles which say that the richest man in America, John Ford had converted to Islam. Hence, the claim made in the post is **FALSE**."[362]

---

[361] Dawa Bisaya, "John Ford, the richest man in America...," Facebook, December 22, 2021, https://www.facebook.com/dawabisaya/posts/4128390439601 87. Accessed October 22, 2024.

[362] Mandadi, "The claim that John Ford," op. cit.

THE DOUBLEMINDEDNESS BEHIND THE FANTASIES

These fantasies manifest a deeply rooted paradox in Islamic attitudes toward the West. On the one hand there is the contempt that the Qur'an inculcates among Muslims—"the best of people" (3:110)—toward the unbelievers, "the most vile of created beings" (98:6), mingled with the suspicion engendered by the warning that "the Jews will not be pleased with you, neither will the Christians, until you follow their religion." (2:120)

At the same time, however, many Muslims clearly had immense regard for the West, and for its distinguished figures—so much admiration, in fact, that prominent Westerners living and dead had to be claimed for Islam. The steady stream of Western converts to Islam wasn't enough, just as no parcel of land, no appropriated Jewish, Christian, or Hindu holy site, was ever enough. The fantasies about prominent converts betrayed an unspoken admiration for the very people that the Qur'an told Muslims to regard with disdain. Otherwise, their imagined conversions wouldn't have generated nearly as much enthusiasm as they did.

If Islam did not create so many failed societies, this sneaking admiration for the West might not exist, and no Muslims would feel any need to manufacture Western converts. Yet that admiration was obviously quite real, much more real than the converts themselves.

CHAPTER SIXTEEN

A RETROGRADE FORCE

HYDROPHOBIA

The fantasies about notable converts to Islam looked even worse in light of the recurring phenomenon of so many actual converts to Islam becoming jihad terrorists.

Virtually all political leaders in the Western world are sure that Islam is good for both individuals and societies. They generally have an unshakeable conviction that Islam is essentially good and to be encouraged in its growth in the US and worldwide—aside from those tragic instances in which it is hijacked by a tiny minority of extremists.

Winston Churchill, however, famously took a different view. After gaining considerable experience with Islam in Muslim lands, he wrote:

> How dreadful are the curses which Mohammedanism lays on its votaries! Besides the fanatical frenzy, which is as dangerous in a man as hydrophobia in a dog, there is this fearful fatalistic

> apathy. The effects are apparent in many countries. Improvident habits, slovenly systems of agriculture, sluggish methods of commerce, and insecurity of property exist wherever the followers of the Prophet rule or live. A degraded sensualism deprives this life of its grace and refinement; the next of its dignity and sanctity. The fact that in Mohammedan law every woman must belong to some man as his absolute property—either as a child, a with, or a concubine—must delay the final extinction of slavery until the faith of Islam has ceased to be a great power among men. Individual Moslems may show splendid qualities. Thousands become the brave and loyal soldiers of the Queen: all know how to die: but the influence of the religion paralyses the social development of those who follow it. No stronger retrograde force exists in the world. Far from being moribund. Mohammedanism is a militant and proselytizing faith. It has already spread throughout Central Africa, raising fearless warriors at every step; and were it not that Christianity is sheltered in the strong arms of science, the science against which it had vainly struggled, the civilisation of modern Europe might fall, as fell the civilisation of ancient Rome.[363]

Today these statements embarrass contemporary Britons, who have been thoroughly indoctrinated in the glories of multiculturalism

363 Winston Spencer Churchill, The River War: An Historical Account of the Reconquest of the Soudan (London: Longmans, Green, and Co., 1899), II: 248–250.

to the degree that in April 2014, Paul Weston, a candidate for political office in Hampshire, was actually arrested "on suspicion of religious/racial harassment" simply for reading Churchill's words aloud during a campaign speech.[364]

Woke multicultural pieties are not only preventing us from asking difficult questions about Muslims and Islam, but they're actively harming people and ruining lives. Arresting people for quoting Churchill doesn't change the possibility that he could have been right, and that while some Muslims, as he said, have "splendid qualities," that doesn't mean that Islam is responsible for forming them.

If Islam may be bad for civilizations, it's undoubtedly tragic for countless individuals.

TURNING TO ISLAM

Mujahida bint Usamah was a British doctor who took full advantage of the educational and career opportunities women have in Western countries. But after becoming devout in her observance of Islam, she gave up her medical career and headed for the Islamic State. The heart-stopping photo on her Twitter feed showed the doctor posing happily with a severed head. Her caption? "Dream job, a terrorist doc."[365]

---

364 Lizzie Parry, "Arrested for quoting Winston Churchill: European election candidate accused of religious and racial harassment after he repeats wartime prime minister's words on Islam during campaign speech," Daily Mail, April 28, 2014, https://www.dailymail.co.uk/news/article-2614834/Arrested-quoting-Winston-Churchill-European-election-candidate-accused-religious-racial-harassment-repeats-wartime-prime-ministers-words-Islam-campaign-speech.html. Accessed October 30, 2024.

365 "British medical student who joined Islamic State poses with severed head," News Corp Australia, September 15, 2014, https://www.news.com.au/world/british-medical-student-who-joined-islamic-state-poses-with-severed-head/news-story/ee70951be15cd1cf819b205f8cd46776. Accessed October 30, 2024.

Maher "Mike" Hawash was a popular and wealthy Intel executive in Portland, Oregon, a pillar of his community and the very model of a moderate, assimilated American Muslim. The *Wall Street Journal* stated that he had "fully integrated himself into the mainstream community where he lived. In many respects he had attained the American dream. He owned his own home and was respected at microchip-maker Intel, one of the U.S.'s preeminent high-tech giants. He was exceptionally popular and known in the community for his volunteer activities."[366]

However, Hawash began to grow devout in his observance of Islam, and as he became more zealous in his observance of the religion, he began to change—until ultimately he served time in prison for recruiting Muslims to join al-Qaeda and the Taliban in Afghanistan.

There are so very many such stories. As far back as 2007, the *New Yorker* magazine summarized just a few among many: "In 2004, Ryan Anderson, a Muslim convert in the Washington Army National Guard, was convicted of attempting to provide Al Qaeda with military intelligence. (During a military sting, Anderson said, 'I wish to defect from the United States. I wish to join Al Qaeda, train its members, and conduct terrorist attacks.') John Walker Lindh, who grew up in Marin County, California, never plotted against America, but he joined and fought for the Taliban."[367]

In London in 2017, a convert to Islam calling himself Khalid Masood killed four people and injured over fifty more in a

366 Scot J. Paltrow, "One Immigrant's Stark Course From Success to Terror Charges," Wall Street Journal, April 29, 2003, https://www.wsj.com/articles/SB105156870497486200. Accessed October 30, 2024.

367 Raffi Khatchadourian, "Azzam the American," New Yorker, January 14, 2007, https://www.newyorker.com/magazine/2007/01/22/azzam-the-american?currentPage=all. Accessed October 30, 2024.

vehicular jihad attack on Westminster Bridge in London. After he drove his car into a crowd, Masood jumped out and murdered a policeman.[368]

Just days after Masood's attack, another convert made news in Detroit. The *Detroit News* reported that "a Detroit man accused of plotting jihad on behalf of the Islamic State accepted a plea deal with federal prosecutors Thursday and could spend up to five years in prison. Sebastian Gregerson admitted he acquired a fragmentation grenade last summer from an undercover FBI employee, a crime because the grenade was an unregistered destructive device."[369]

One more new Muslim appeared in a German court the week after that. A convert to Islam whom the German media identified as Marco G. was judged to be guilty "of attempted murder for placing an explosive device at the main train station in the western city of Bonn in December 2012."[370]

A few days after that, AFP reported that a "New Jersey teen pleaded guilty…to a plot allegedly inspired by the Islamic State group to kill Pope Francis during his 2015 visit to the United States. The US Justice Department said Santos Colon, fifteen years old at the time, sought to recruit a sniper to shoot the pope as he celebrated mass in Philadelphia on September 27, 2015.

---

368 Zoie O'Brien, "'No evidence' Westminster terrorist Khalid Masood linked to ISIS - Met Police," Express, March 27, 2017, https://www.express.co.uk/news/uk/784526/Westminster-London-terror-attack-ISIS-claims-terror-Khalid-Masood-Adrian-Elms-Met-Police. Accessed October 30, 2024.

369 Robert Snell, "Detroit terror suspect strikes deal in federal court," Detroit News, March 30, 2017, https://www.detroitnews.com/story/news/local/detroit-city/2017/03/30/detroit-terror-suspect-plea/99819196/. Accessed October 30, 2024.

370 Frank Jordans, "German court sentences extremist to life over bomb plot," Associated Press, April 3, 2017, https://apnews.com/general-news-a80f6850ed4e4e4eb4d4ff-7d0ac24396. Accessed October 30, 2024.

Colon also allegedly planned to set off explosives."[371] "Santos Colon" is not the name Muslim parents would give a child; Colon was yet another lethal convert to Islam.

On December 8, 2020, a Cuban-born convert to Islam in south Florida, Jonathan Guerra Blanco, was arrested and charged with providing material support to ISIS. According to the FBI, Guerra produced propaganda videos and guides in order to "incite and equip primarily Spanish-speaking followers to conduct operational attacks in support of ISIS."[372] Guerra "produced and distributed an ISIS video titled 'Called to Islam' that featured a Spanish-language video 'threatening non-believers to convert to Islam.' Among the video footage were shots of the Biltmore Hotel in Coral Gables and the Las Vegas Strip, along with clips of a suicide bomber's farewell address and a prisoner execution."[373] Guerra said that he wanted to "make the word of Allah…the highest," and added: "I always strive to please Allah. I don't want to brag, but I dedicate my life to [jihad]."[374]

In January 2021, the Justice Department announced that Texas resident Jaylyn Christopher Molina, "aka Abdur Rahim, admitted to conspiring to provide material support to the designated foreign terrorist organization Islamic State of Iraq and al-Sham/Syria (ISIS)."[375]

---

371 "US teen pleads guilty to IS-inspired plot to kill pope," Agence France-Presse, April 3, 2017, https://www.breitbart.com/news/us-teen-pleads-guilty-to-is-inspired-plot-to-kill-pope/. Accessed October 30, 2024.

372 Jay Weaver, "Florida man seeks plea deal after being charged with backing terror group ISIS," Miami Herald, December 8, 2020, https://www.miamiherald.com/news/local/article247673625.html. Accessed October 30, 2024.

373 Ibid.

374 Ibid.

375 "Texas Man Pleads Guilty to Conspiracy to Provide Material Support to ISIS," US Department of Justice, January 25, 2021, https://www.justice.gov/opa/pr/texas-man-pleads-guilty-conspiracy-provide-material-support-isis. Accessed October 30, 2024.

Some of these dangerous converts have become quite prominent. Adam Gadahn, an American from Oregon, became a top al-Qaeda operative; he was killed in an American drone strike in 2015. A 2007 *New Yorker* profile of Gadahn notes that he was "the first American to be charged with treason in more than fifty years" and he executed his duties as an al-Qaeda spokesman with "tremendous conviction."[376] The story lists a few other prominent jihadis who were converts to Islam: "Jose Padilla (the so-called Dirty Bomber) and Richard Reid (the so-called Shoe Bomber) are well-known examples."[377]

The author of the *New Yorker* profile of Gadahn, Raffi Khatchadourian, says that Americans who convert to Islam and turn to terror "are especially rare and are poorly understood; most of the scholarship about them is only a few years old. And yet, because of their cultural literacy, and because of the mobility that their citizenship provides, they are potentially the most dangerous of terrorists."[378] Accordingly, "a small number of specialists" have begun "to search for a pattern behind homegrown radicalization and recruitment."[379] In doing so, however, they seem to have studied everything but Islam: "Their research has led them to examine the sociology of cults, the psychology of fanaticism, even the formation of defunct political terror groups like West Germany's Red Army Faction."[380] This was in keeping with the near-universal Western assumption that Islam was fundamentally peaceful, and that therefore a convert to Islam who embraced violence must be influenced by factors other than Islam that could be observed in other context.

376 Khatchadourian, "Azzam the American," op. cit.
377 Ibid.
378 Ibid.
379 Ibid.
380 Ibid.

Khatchadourian consults an FBI agent, Randy Parsons, who confirms this false assumption, explaining, "The thing that concerns me with Adam Gadahn's situation is, how did it happen? How did he convert, not to Islam, because obviously what he is into is not mainstream Islam, but to a particularly virulent, violent, radical view of Islam? How does somebody get to that?"

A READER OF THE QUR'AN

Parsons can't conceive of the possibility that Gadahn may have come to his "virulent, violent, radical view of Islam" simply by reading the Qur'an and studying Islam. Parsons evidently thought that if Gadahn had done that, he would have embraced "mainstream Islam," which he assumed to be peaceful and tolerant. He, and the FBI in general, would have done well to study the case of Mohammed Reza Taheri-azar, who was not a convert to Islam, but an irreligious Muslim who decided to change his behavior and follow the tenets of his religion. On March 3, 2006, Taheri-azar, who was a student at the University of North Carolina at Chapel Hill, rented an SUV and drove it onto campus, trying to kill as many students as he could.

Taheri-azar killed no one, but he did injure nine people. In court later, he said he was "thankful for the opportunity to spread the will of Allah."[381] He wrote a detailed letter attempting to explain his actions, ascribing them entirely to his newfound Islamic faith: "In the name of Allah, the merciful, the compassionate. To whom it may concern: I am writing this letter to inform you of my reasons for premeditating and attempting to

381 "UNC Grad in Court on Alleged Hit and Run," Associated Press, March 6, 2006, https://www.foxnews.com/story/unc-grad-in-court-on-alleged-hit-and-run. Accessed October 30, 2024.

murder citizens and residents of the United States of America on Friday, March 3, 2006 in the city of Chapel Hill, North Carolina by running them over with my automobile and stabbing them with a knife if the opportunities are presented to me by Allah."[382]

Taheri-azar identified himself simply as a "servant of Allah." He explained that "in the Qur'an, Allah states that the believing men and women have permission to murder anyone responsible for the killing of other believing men and women.... After extensive contemplation and reflection, I have made the decision to exercise the right of violent retaliation that Allah has given me to the fullest extent to which I am capable at present."[383]

In another letter the following week, Taheri-azar elaborated on his Islamic inspiration: "I live with the holy Koran as my constitution for right and wrong and definition of justice.... Allah gives permission in the Koran for the followers of Allah to attack those who have raged [sic] war against them, with the expectation of eternal paradise in case of martyrdom and/or living one's life in obedience of all of Allah's commandments found throughout the Koran's 114 chapters. I've read all 114 chapters approximately 15 times since June of 2003 when I started reading the Koran."[384]

Taheri-azar maintained that his attempt at mass murder was a matter of his Islamic practice, for he did not act "out of hatred for Americans, but out of love for Allah instead. I live only to serve Allah, by obeying all of Allah's commandments of which I am aware by reading and learning the contents of the Koran."[385]

---

382 "A Terrorist's Letter," Herald Sun, March 27, 2006, https://www.leatherneck.com/forums/showthread.php?27915-A-Terrorist-s-Letter&s=970d4f87b4934e27d2367d1127d49f03. Accessed October 30, 2024.

383 Ibid.

384 Robert Spencer, "Killing for Allah," FrontPageMagazine.com, March 29, 2006, https://swap.stanford.edu/was/20090618203455/http://www.frontpagemagazine.com/readArticle.aspx?ARTID=5032. Accessed October 30, 2024.

385 Ibid.

Taheri-azar also sent a detailed explanation of what the Qur'an taught about warfare against unbelievers to the UNC-Chapel Hill campus newspaper,[386] presenting extensive Qur'anic evidence for his positions, such as: "Allah demands of believers to retaliate violently against persons responsible for attacking them or their fellow Believers around the world. ([Qur'an] 2:178–179, 5:45, 8:72, 9:38, 9:71, 42:39–42, 49:10)."[387] These letters were noteworthy for being entirely the result of his own study. He says nothing about having been involved with campus Islamic groups, and does not seem to have been. He was not known to have frequented the local mosque. He presented his conclusion that Allah required him as a believer to do violence to unbelievers entirely as the result of his study of the Qur'an.

For Randy Parsons and other FBI agents, such a conclusion was inconceivable. Mohammed Reza Taheri-azar must have missed all of the Qur'an's peaceful teachings. And Adam Gadahn must have had non-Islamic influences that contributed to his "radicalization." The *New Yorker* profile of the future al-Qaeda spokesman, however, suggests just the opposite.

"A REVOLTING GEEK OF MASS PROPORTIONS"

Adam Gadahn, according to Raffi Khatchadourian, grew up on a California farm, the children of hippies who dabbled in Christianity. As a teen, he discovered death metal music and the subculture around it, but still felt a "void," and began looking into Christianity again, as well as Islam.[388] He described him-

386 Robert Spencer, "Letters from a mujahid," Jihad Watch, May 12, 2006, https://jihadwatch.org/2006/05/letters-from-a-mujahid. Accessed October 30, 2024.

387 Ibid.

388 Raffi Khatchadourian, "Azzam the American," op. cit.

self in a letter to a fellow death metal fan as "revolting geek of mass proportions."[389] Soon afterward, however, he converted to Islam under the auspices of Dr. Muzammil Siddiqi of the Islamic Society of Orange County in Garden Grove, California.

The former president of the Islamic Society of North America, Siddiqi's conspicuously non-moderate statements had raised eyebrows more than once. He said in 2004 that "in some cases a husband may use some light disciplinary action in order to correct the moral infraction of his wife.... The Koran is very clear on this issue."[390]

It is indeed. The Qur'an says, "Men are in charge of women, because Allah has made the one superior to the other, and because they spend of their property. So good women are obedient, guarding in secret what Allah has guarded. As for those from whom you fear disobedience, give them a warning and banish them to separate beds, and beat them." (4:34) Most Westerners, however, were unaware of this passage, and Islamic spokesmen in the US generally ignored it, at least when facing non-Muslim audiences. Siddiqi was a notable exception.

Siddiqi nonetheless enjoyed great respect among non-Muslim authorities; he even participated, at the invitation of President George W. Bush, in the National Day of Prayer after the September 11 jihad attacks. On that occasion, he said, "I believe that as Muslims we should participate in the [American] system to safeguard our interests and try to bring gradual change.... We must not forget that Allah's rules have to be established in

389 Ibid.

390 Steven Stalinsky and Y. Yehoshua, "Muslim Clerics on the Religious Rulings Regarding Wife-Beating," MEMRI, Special Report No. 27, March 22, 2004, https://www.memri.org/reports/muslim-clerics-religious-rulings-regarding-wife-beating, Accessed October 30, 2024.

all lands, and all our efforts should lead to that direction."[391] No one present seems to have been interested in exploring the implications of this statement. The pundit Charles Krauthammer, however, did notice that Siddiqi had said nothing about the 9/11 attacks being against Islam.

With long experience in the public eye, Siddiqi knew how to couch his statements so as not to arouse concern. When Raffi Khatchadourian asked him to define jihad, Siddiqi responded that it was "a struggle for peace and justice, so that you establish peace in the world, you establish justice in the world, and defend your own rights—the right of life, the right of property, the right of dignity and honor and freedom, and the right of your religion. So you defend yourself for that, and you defend other people who are suffering and oppressed. So jihad may take a military action, but it is not always a military action."[392] Whether or not Khatchadourian was aware of it, Siddiqi's statement was about not just establishing "peace in the world," but about securing the hegemony of Islam ("the right of your religion"). Qutb and Maududi would have approved.

Gadahn, however, wrote an essay soon after his conversion, in which he asserted that Muslims were "not the bloodthirsty, barbaric terrorists that the news media and the televangelists paint them to be."[393] Yet ultimately, that was what he turned into, due to his study of the Qur'an and Sunnah.

---

391 Robert Reilly, "The Muddled Catholic-Muslim 'Dialogue,'" The Catholic Thing, March 21, 2016, https://www.thecatholicthing.org/2016/03/21/the-muddled-catholic-muslim-dialogue/. Accessed October 30, 2024.

392 Raffi Khatchadourian, "Azzam the American," op. cit.

393 Ibid.

CHAPTER SEVENTEEN

ADVENTURES OF THE DEVOUT

"I HAD EVERYTHING IN THE WORLD"

On May 1, 2010, Faisal Shahzad, who had once worked as a financial analyst, tried to set off a car bomb on a busy Saturday night in Times Square. Shahzad and his bomb were discovered before he could do any harm, but he made his motives and intentions clear in a video he recorded before he ventured into the heart of New York City. Shahzad explained, "I had everything in the world. I had a nice car. I had a house. I had an excellent job. They were paying me good money. But deep inside I always had this thought that there's probably more than this to life."[394] He therefore turned to Islam. Shahzad asserted that "jihad, holy fighting in Allah's cause, with full force of numbers and weaponry, is given the utmost importance in Islam.... By jihad, Islam is established.... By abandoning jihad, may Allah

394 "Attacks, Attempts Show Cost of Radicalization," IPT News, March 4, 2011, https://www.investigativeproject.org/2651/attacks-attempts-show-cost-of-radicalization. Accessed October 30, 2024.

protect us from that, Islam is destroyed, and Muslims go into inferior position, their honor is lost, their lands are stolen, their rule and authority vanish. Jihad is an obligation and duty in Islam on every Muslim."[395]

Shahzad was confident that he would be one of many jihadis attacking the US, and all other infidel polities, until the vision of Qutb and Maududi came to fruition and Islamic rule was established all over the world: "You will see that the Muslim world has just started.... Islam is coming to the world, inshallah, Islam will spread on the whole world. And the democracy will be defeated, and so was Communism defeated, and all the others isms and schisms will be defeated, and the word of Allah will be supreme, inshallah. And Muslims are gonna do that. And as Allah says in sura 3, verse 110 [of the Qur'an]..." Qur'an 3:110 says: "You are the best of people that has been raised up for mankind. You command what is right and forbid what is wrong, and you believe in Allah. And if the people of the book had believed, it would have been better for them. Some of them are believers, but most of them are rebellious."

"STEP BY STEP I BECAME A RELIGIOUSLY DEVOUT MUSLIM"

In the mid-2000s, a young man named Carlos Leon Bledsoe in Little Rock, Arkansas converted to Islam, changing his name to Abdulhakim Mujahid Muhammad. The *New York Times* stated, "A gentle, happy-go-lucky teenager, he had become a deeply observant Muslim in college, shunning gatherings where alcohol

395 "Taliban Video of Faisal Shahzad," New York Times, September 29, 2010, https://www.nytimes.com/video/nyregion/1248069111343/taliban-video-of-faisal-shahzad.html. Accessed October 29, 2024.

was served."[396] On June 1, 2009, he carried out what he referred to as a "random and unplanned attack" at a US military recruitment center in his home city. He shot two soldiers whom he saw outside the recruitment center, explaining, "I did not want them to see me coming. I had the SKS with me and put it out the window. I rolled by and started shooting. I was trying to kill them."[397] He did kill one of them; he wounded the other.

Bledsoe/Muhammad later explained how "step by step I became a religiously devout Muslim, Mujahid—meaning one who participates in jihad."[398] He said that "in Islam there's a call to duty—jihad—and it's of different types but the one I'm mentioning is a defensive struggle or fight with weapons against those who attack, kill, maim the Muslims. And this is a part of Islam."[399]

The zealous young convert added, "Far as Al-Qaeda in the Arabian Peninsula I won't say much but yes, I'm affiliated with them. And it's more of a Islamic Revivalist Revolutionary Movement than an organization. Same with other Al-Qaeda fronts. Our goal is to rid the Islamic world of idols and idolaters, paganism and pagans, infidelity and infidels, hypocrisy and hypocrites, apostasy and apostates, democracy and democrats and relaunch the Islamic caliphate...and to establish Islamic law (Shari'ah)—Allah's law on earth and anyone who strives for this is affiliated with the movement. So yes I'm Al Qaeda and proud to be."[400]

---

396 James Dao, "A Muslim Son, a Murder Trial and Many Questions," New York Times, February 16, 2010, https://www.nytimes.com/2010/02/17/us/17convert.html. Accessed October 29, 2024.

397 Kristina Goetz, "Memphian drifted to dark side of Islamic extremism, plotted one-man jihad vs. homeland," Memphis Commercial Appeal, November 24, 2010. https://archive.knoxnews.com/news/state/muslim-who-shot-soldier-in-arkansas-says-he-wanted-to-cause-more-death-ep-407169853-358338211.html. Accessed October 29, 2024.

398 Ibid.

399 Ibid.

400 Ibid.

"My heart bleeds for the families of the victims," said Abdulhakim Mujahid Muhammad's father, Melvin Bledsoe. "Evildoers," he said, had "brainwashed" his son while the FBI stood by idly. "They didn't pull the trigger," said Melvin Bledsoe, "but they allowed this to happen. It is owed to the American people to know what happened. If it can happen to my son, it can happen to anyone's son."[401] His son agreed: "In regards to the CIA & FBI yea they followed me, yea they tapped my phone, read my emails, interrogated me not once, not twice but three times before my jihadi attack on the crusader recruiting center but what good did it do? I outsmarted them and they know it."[402]

The former Carlos Bledsoe further gloated, "I know the real reason why they're so (quiet). And it's because they dropped the ball with me and not just me. Nidal (Malik Hasan, the U.S. Army major charged in the Fort Hood shootings), Umar Farouk (the Nigerian charged for trying to detonate plastic explosives on a Northwest Airlines flight), Faisal (Shahzad, the Pakistani-American sentenced to life in prison for his failed attempt to bomb Times Square) and others who evaded their agents and devices and paid-informants posing as Muslims. They can't catch us all."[403]

Abdulhakim Mujahid Muhammad expressed regret only that he had not been able to pull off a larger jihad attack: "Compared to what I had planned originally it was like a grain of sand. One crusader dead, one wounded, 15 terrorized, big deal. Nidal Malik (Hasan, the accused Fort Hood shooter) is the real Islamic warrior, and my plan A was on that scale."[404] Nevertheless, he

401 Dao, "A Muslim Son," op. cit.
402 Goetz, "Memphian drifted," op. cit.
403 Ibid.
404 Ibid.

had hope for the future: "I'm just one Muhammad. There are millions of Muhammads out there. And I hope and pray the next one be more deadlier than Muhammad Atta!! (peace be upon him) commander of the blessed raids in NY and D.C. on 9/11."[405]

Abdulhakim Mujahid Muhammad's long-suffering father, Melvin Bledsoe, was right: this can happen to anyone, and it's very clear why the FBI and CIA allowed it to happen: it would have been "Islamophobic" to take any step at all that might give anyone the impression that Islam was not a religion like any other, part of America's rich and glorious mosaic of religions and cultures.

"I KNOW WHAT I DID WAS WRONG AND I'M SORRY"

The same thing that happened to Carlos Bledsoe happened to another young American, Trevor Bickford.

When Trevor Bickford was nineteen years old, on December 31, 2022, he ventured to Times Square along with multitudes of New Year's Eve revelers, but he was not interested in joining the festivities. Instead, he attacked three NYPD officers with a machete. In January 2024, he pleaded guilty to three charges of attempted murder, and while his motive was abundantly clear, authorities characteristically appeared to be completely indifferent about what its implications were for the future.

Bickford, who had come down to Times Square from his home in Wells, Maine, said as he entered his guilty plea, "On Dec. 31, 2022, I attempted to kill three NYPD officers with a knife while they were working in Manhattan. I know what I did

[405] Ibid.

was wrong and I'm sorry."[406] It would have been more helpful if young Bickford had explained why exactly he was sorry now for an act that he carried out in accord with his newfound beliefs and ideology.

The Associated Press stated that Bickford "shouted 'Allahu akbar'—the Arabic phrase for God is great—before striking the officers in the head with the machete and trying to grab an officer's gun, authorities said. One officer suffered a fractured skull."[407] Yet again, AP's explanation was inaccurate: "Allahu akbar" doesn't mean "God is great"; it actually means "Allah is greater." That is, the god of Islam is superior to anything that non-Muslims worship or hold dear. As we have seen, this declaration of superiority frequently accompanies acts that are designed to enforce the subjugation and submission of the non-believer or "infidel," amounting to a kind of explanation of why a particular act of violence is being perpetrated. Nevertheless, it was unusually forthright of the far-left news service to mention the inconvenient fact that Bickford shouted this at all. AP even went so far as to add that "authorities say he had studied radical Islamic ideology and decided to wage jihad against U.S. officials."[408] Yet while AP was frank about Bickford's motive, Bickford himself appeared to be trying to obscure it. "At the outset of the hearing," AP tells us, "Bickford said he was taking three medications for treatment of schizoaffective disorder." (In Europe, it is extremely common for clear cases of jihad violence to be dismissed as mental illness, with the perpetrators hospitalized rather than imprisoned.)

---

406 "Maine man pleads guilty in New Year's Eve machete attack near Times Square," Associated Press, January 11, 2024, https://apnews.com/article/new-years-eve-machete-bickford-f58a19ff25b7d823b216ebb7277637ce. Accessed October 30, 2024.

407 Ibid.

408 Ibid.

There was no doubt, however, when Bickford was arrested. In his backpack was a handwritten note, asking his family to "please repent to Allah and accept Islam."[409] To his mother, Bickford wrote, "I fear greatly that you will not repent to Allah. And therefore I hold hope in my heart that a piece of you believes so that you may be taken out to [sic] the hellfire."[410] To his brother, he likewise wrote, "Please repent to Allah and accept Islam. I fear for you." To another brother in the Marines, he added, "You have joined the ranks of my enemy. And for that I can give you no kind words—return to Allah."[411]

As Bickford pleaded guilty, Assistant US Attorney Sarah Kushner said that there was "'no doubt' that he attacked the officers because they were military-age men.... She said Bickford had intended to kill 'as many as possible' of the men in uniform that he came across."[412] She added that he had "originally intended to go overseas and fight alongside terrorists there but eventually decided to carry out an attack in the United States instead. She said he told investigators that he had walked around Times Square before the attack, 'trying to figure out the right time to kill.'"[413]

The big question that remains is where Trevor Bickford, who had converted to Islam not long before his machete attack, learned all this. Was it at a mosque? Was it from Muslims in his area?

---

409 Joe Marino and Jorge Fitz-Gibbon, "Alleged Islamic extremist in machete attack on NYPD cops asked family to 'repent to Allah' in disturbing manifesto," New York Post, January 1, 2023, https://nypost.com/2023/01/01/suspect-in-nyc-cop-attack-wrote-disturbing-manifesto-sources/. Accessed October 30, 2024.

410 Ibid.

411 Ibid.

412 "Maine Man," Associated Press, op. cit.

413 Ibid.

Authorities should have studied carefully what they were almost certainly ignoring, such as the questions of how and where this young man converted to Islam, and how he got the idea that his new religion, which non-Muslim authorities all over the Western world assure us is completely peaceful and tolerant, commanded him to consider non-Muslims enemies and violently attack them.

These questions are never asked, much less answered, despite the fact that converts to Islam turning to jihad violence is a distressingly common phenomenon. American intelligence and law enforcement officials don't want to do anything to give the impression that they don't accept the dogma that Islam is a religion of peace and tolerance that has nothing whatsoever to do with terrorism. The fact that converts to Islam such as Trevor Bickford have somehow gotten exactly the opposite idea doesn't ever make authorities pause and reflect upon their core assumptions.

"KILL AS MANY PEOPLE AS POSSIBLE"

Sunday, April 7, 2024, was just another day in the fair city of Coeur d'Alene, Idaho. But if a teenager named Alexander Scott Mercurio had gotten his way, it would have gone down in history as another one of those infamous dates, akin to December 7, September 11, and October 7. Instead, Mercurio was arrested before he could carry out his murderous plans. Nevertheless, he showed—as unmistakably as did Carlos Bledsoe, Trevor Bickford, and so many others—why it was unwise to let the case of this bloody-minded young man pass unnoticed.

CNN reported that Mercurio had "planned to attack churches in Coeur d'Alene, Idaho, on Sunday 'using weapons, including knives, firearms, and fire,' according to court documents cited by the Justice Department."[414] He wrote out his plan: "Stop close by the church, equip the weapon(s) and storm the temple, kill as many people as possible before they inevitably disperse/scatter, then burn the temple to the ground and flee the scene."[415] He planned improbably to repeat this scenario at all twenty-one churches in Coeur d'Alene; what he imagined the local police might be doing in all the time it would have taken to do this is unclear.

Another convert to Islam, Alexander Scott Mercurio wanted to commit this large-scale mass murder because of his Islamic faith and loyalty to the Islamic State (ISIS), was and anxious to demonstrate the fervor of his new faith by carrying out his massacre during the holy month of Ramadan.

Western analysts routinely tell us that Ramadan is a time when many Muslims try to intensify their devotion to Allah, and that's true. A hadith has a Muslim asking Muhammad, "Instruct me as to such a deed as equals Jihad (in reward)." Muhammad replied, "I do not find such a deed." (Bukhari 4.52.44) So what better way to increase one's devotion to Allah than by waging jihad? In April 2022, the Palestinian Authority's Supreme Sharia Judge, Mahmoud Al-Habbash, declared that "Ramadan is not a month of laziness but rather a month of activity, of effort, and of hard work, and as it also was in the life of the Prophet, a month

[414] Jack Forrest, "FBI arrests man who allegedly pledged allegiance to ISIS and planned attacks on Idaho churches, DOJ says," CNN, April 9, 2024, https://www.cnn.com/2024/04/08/politics/fbi-arrest-man-isis-churches-idaho/index.html. Accessed October 29, 2024.

[415] Patrick Smith, "Idaho teen arrested and accused of planning to kill churchgoers in the name of ISIS," NBC News, April 9, 2024, https://www.nbcnews.com/news/us-news/idaho-teen-arrested-plan-kill-churchgoers-isis-inspired-attack-rcna146958. Accessed October 29, 2024.

of jihad, conquest, and victory."[416] Every Ramadan, therefore, we see an increase in jihad attacks.

The pious young man "stated he intended to incapacitate his father with a pipe, handcuff him, and use the firearms locked in the closet to attack the church."[417] He explained that he wanted to attack his father because his parents were not happy with his "deen"—that is, his religion. As the Qur'an says, "You will not find people who believe in Allah and the last day loving those who oppose Allah and his messenger, even though they be their fathers or their sons or their brothers or their tribe." (58:22)

Mercurio was frustrated that he had not yet had a chance to demonstrate his zeal: "I am a hypocrite who has not even spat in the face of a kafir [non-believer] or donated a single penny in the cause of Allah, let alone spilled their blood and induced terror into their hearts and minds."[418] (This also is a statement inspired by the Qur'an, which instructs Muslims to "strike terror in the enemies of Allah." (8:60)) To express his devotion to his "deen," Mercurio made a video holding a knife and standing in front of an ISIS flag, pledging his allegiance to the jihad group. In his parents' home, where he lived (of course), there were "items consistent with his planned attack," including a "metal pipe, handcuffs, folding saw, head coverings, two cannisters of butane fuel, and machete," as well as "multiple rifles and handguns."[419]

Authorities warned that Mercurio is an example of the "dangers of self-radicalization," but again ignored the material that radicalized him. The recurring pattern of converts to Islam somehow getting the idea that their new religion requires them

---

416 Maurice Hirsch, "The PA/Fatah initiated and fueled terror wave," Palestinian Media Watch, April 10, 2022, https://palwatch.org/page/31033. Accessed October 29, 2024.

417 Smith, "Idaho teen," op. cit.

418 Smith, "Idaho teen," op. cit.

419 Forrest, "FBI arrests man," op. cit.

to do violence to non-Muslims has never been of the slightest concern to intelligence or law enforcement officials in the US or anywhere else. The fact that no officials want to face is that some reading material is more conducive to "self-radicalization" than others; Mercurio, didn't undergo his "self-radicalization" while reading Dr. Seuss. Such considerations could lead to "Islamophobia," and those who have the responsibility to protect American citizens have clearly decided that it is better that Americans be murdered in jihad attacks than that the root cause of these "self-radicalizations" be examined.

CHAPTER EIGHTEEN

'JUST A BIG TEDDY BEAR'

"A BIG TEDDY BEAR"

Edward Schimenti of the Chicago suburb of Zion, Illinois, wanted you to know that he was "just a big teddy bear"; he said so during his sentencing hearing in April 2021, when he got thirteen and a half years for aiding the Islamic State (ISIS), joining the long and ever-lengthening list of converts to Islam who turn to terrorism, even in the United States.

According to the Justice Department, "evidence at trial revealed that Schimenti advocated on social media for violent extremism in support of the terrorist group. In 2015, Schimenti began meeting with undercover FBI employees and individuals who, unbeknownst to Schimenti, were cooperating with law enforcement. During the meetings, Schimenti discussed his devotion to ISIS and his commitment to ISIS principles."[420] A true believer, he wrote, "Islamic State will control your country, matter of fact, Islam will dominate the world!!"[421] Sayyid Qutb and Sayyid Abul A'la Maududi would have been pleased to hear him say so. AP noted that Schimenti's Google Plus profile showed "a masked man holding a knife and standing alongside an IS flag. A caption reads in capital letters that if you can't travel abroad to fight, 'then slaughter the pagans next to you.'"[422]

Schimenti didn't just talk. As the Justice Department explained, two FBI informants posing as ISIS operatives met with Schimenti. After initially being suspicious enough to leave a meeting abruptly, Schimenti fell for the ruse. The Justice Department noted that "in 2017, Schimenti furnished cellular phones to one of the cooperating individuals, believing the phones would be used to detonate explosive devices in ISIS attacks overseas. On April 7, 2017, Schimenti drove with the cooperating individual to O'Hare International Airport in Chicago, with the understanding that the cooperating individual would be traveling to Syria to fight with ISIS."[423] Schimenti told him to "drench that land with they, they blood." On another occasion, he declared, "I want to see blood flowing, either way."[424]

---

420 "Suburban Chicago Man Sentenced to More Than 13 Years in Prison for Conspiring to Provide Material Support to ISIS," US Department of Justice, April 9, 2021, https://www.justice.gov/usao-ndil/pr/suburban-chicago-man-sentenced-more-13-years-prison-conspiring-provide-material-support. Accessed October 30, 2024.

421 Jon Seidel, "Zion man gets more than 13 years in prison for conspiracy to support Islamic State, telling informant 'I want to see blood flowing,'" Chicago Sun-Times, April 9, 2021, https://chicago.suntimes.com/politics/2021/4/9/22375978/zion-man-prison-conspiracy-support-islamic-state-schimenti-jones-dirksen. Accessed October 30, 2024.

422 "2 suburban Chicago men arrested on terrorism charges," Associated Press, April 12, 2017, https://www.foxnews.com/us/2-suburban-chicago-men-arrested-on-terrorism-charges. Accessed October 30, 2024.

423 "Suburban Chicago Man," Department of Justice, op. cit.

424 Seidel, "Zion man," op. cit.

Previously, according to the *Chicago Sun-Times*, "Schimenti helped the informant get into fighting shape at a gym, prosecutors said. There, they said Schimenti said he hoped to be the one to 'cut the neck' of non-believers."[425] And the *Chicago Tribune* reported in March that "although the charges do not allege the two participated in any violence, Schimenti talked with the informant about future plans to attack Naval Station Great Lakes in North Chicago, a short distance from his home."[426]

Also in April 2017, Schimenti went to Illinois Beach Park in Zion with another convert to Islam, Joseph D. Jones. They took with them an Islamic State flag, and at the park posed for photos while holding it, to the alarm of passersby. There turned out to be quite a bit to be alarmed about; in the course of the investigation of the two men, it came to light that Schimenti had threatened a gay man with Sharia punishments, telling him that once Islamic law came to the United States, "We are putting you (homosexuals) on top of Sears Tower (now the Willis Tower) and we drop you."[427]

In planning to cut the necks of unbelievers, Schimenti believed he was fulfilling the command of Allah: "When you meet the unbelievers, strike the necks" (Qur'an 47:4). In his piety and desire to be pleasing to his deity, his bloodlust could have been more a fulfillment of a religious duty than arising out of a heart inclined to hatred and violence. The Qur'an itself even envisions this possibility when it says, "Fighting is prescribed for

---

425 Ibid.

426 Jason Meisner, "Zion man sentenced to 12 years in federal prison for conspiring to assist ISIS," Chicago Tribune, March 4, 2021, https://www.chicagotribune.com/2021/03/03/zion-man-sentenced-to-12-years-in-federal-prison-for-conspiring-to-assist-isis/. Accessed October 30, 2024.

427 "Chicago men charged with trying to join Islamic State after FBI sting," Times of Israel, April 13, 2017, https://www.timesofisrael.com/chicago-men-charged-with-trying-to-join-islamic-state-after-fbi-sting/. Accessed October 30, 2024.

you, though you dislike it." (2:216) Schimenti may have really disliked it, but he disliked angering Allah even more.

"I DO BELIEVE THAT I DESERVE THE MAXIMUM SENTENCE"

Maybe it was just a play for sympathy or an attempt to prove that he was remorseful, but when former US Army Private Cole Bridges appeared in court in October 2024 to be sentenced for plotting to aid Islamic State jihadis in carrying out massacres in the United States, as well as ambushing and murdering his fellow soldiers, he actually requested the maximum forty-year sentence. Bridges appears to have realized the disastrous course his life has taken, but would military and intelligence officials absorb the lessons of his case? That remained unlikely.

Bridges got a sentence of fourteen years, rather than forty, despite telling Judge Lewis J. Liman, "Honestly, I do believe that I deserve the maximum sentence. I know what I did was wrong."[428] He added that he would feel "regret for as long as I live."[429]

In September 2019, Bridges joined the Army; he became a cavalry scout for the Third Infantry Division in Fort Stewart, Georgia. However, the seeds of his personal disaster had already been planted. Fox News noted that "about a year before he joined the Army, Bridges began researching and consuming

---

[428] Michael Dorgan, "Army soldier sentenced to 14 years for ISIS plot to kill US forces, after requesting he serve 40 years," Fox News, October 12, 2024, https://www.foxnews.com/us/army-soldier-sentenced-14-years-isis-plot-kill-us-forces-after-requesting-he-serve-40-years. Accessed October 30, 2024.

[429] Ibid.

online propaganda promoting jihadists and their violent ideology, and began to express his support for ISIS and jihad on social media."[430]

After he had been in the army for roughly a year, he "began communicating with an FBI online covert employee (OCE), who was posing as an ISIS supporter in contact with ISIS fighters in the Middle East,"[431] in which he "expressed his frustration with the U.S. military and his desire to aid ISIS."[432]

Nor did he just talk. "Bridges provided training and guidance to purported ISIS fighters who were planning attacks, including advice about potential targets in New York City. He also provided the OCE with portions of a U.S. Army training manual and guidance about military combat tactics, with the understanding that the materials would be used by ISIS in future attack planning."[433]

Even that wasn't all. Around December 2020, according to the Justice Department, Bridges gave his ISIS contact "instructions for the purported ISIS fighters on how to attack U.S. forces in the Middle East."[434] He "diagrammed specific military maneuvers intended to help ISIS fighters maximize the lethality of attacks on U.S. troops"[435] and "provided advice about the best way to fortify an ISIS encampment to repel an attack by U.S. Special Forces, including by wiring certain buildings with explosives to kill the U.S. troops."[436]

---

430 Ibid.

431 Ibid.

432 Ibid.

433 Ibid.

434 "U.S. Army Soldier Pleads Guilty To Terrorism Charges For Attempting To Assist ISIS To Conduct Deadly Ambush On U.S. Troops," US Department of Justice, June 14, 2023, https://www.justice.gov/opa/pr/us-army-soldier-sentenced-14-years-prison-attempting-assist-isis-conduct-deadly-ambush-us. Accessed October 30, 2024.

435 Ibid.

436 Ibid.

Warming to his role, Bridge made a video of himself, which he passed on to his contact, in which he wears army body armor while "standing in front of a flag often used by ISIS fighters and making a gesture symbolic of support for ISIS."[437] He also sent along "a propaganda speech in support of the anticipated ambush by ISIS on U.S. troops."[438]

It's good that he got caught, but once again the one no one dared to ask the most important question: what got into Cole Bridges? The reason why no one was asking this question was that there were two answers, both of which involved hard truths that no one wanted to hear. The first and most obvious answer was that Bridges went from US soldier to traitor because of Islam. Pointing it out will get you swift charges of "Islamophobia"—which is why no one dares discuss such matters—but Islamic theology includes the concept of the *umma*, the supranational community of believers to whom every Muslim theoretically owes an allegiance that is above all other allegiances except to Allah himself.

Thus when Cole Bridges became a Muslim, he was likely told that his identity as an American came second to his identity as a Muslim. That was not necessarily problematic; innumerable Christians think the same thing about Christianity. But he was also probably informed that America, by attacking Muslims in Afghanistan and Iraq, and by supporting Israel, had become an enemy of Islam, such that it was his duty as a Muslim to wage jihad against it.

The second answer to the question of what got into Cole Bridges was just as unwelcome: America got into him. Our

437 Ibid.
438 Ibid.

leftist-dominated, rootless, materialistic, narcissistic, self-obsessed, reality-denying society is leading increasing numbers of young people to think that something, anything, that provides some standards and expectations will be better. Yet with the churches all too often hanging up Pride flags and aping the secular culture, many are finding Islam's absolute unwillingness to compromise with the spirit of the age refreshing.

The problem is that part of Islam's rejection of our society's values is an aggressive and supremacist impulse that leads many believers to want to do violence to unbelievers, to compel them to convert or submit as inferiors to Islamic hegemony. If our culture had any sane values, this might not appear so attractive, but sane values are increasingly hard to come by.

"DEATH TO JEWS"

One convert to Islam who almost became another beneficiary of the prevailing insanity and refusal to face unpleasant facts was Joshua Robles, a sixteen-year-old in Las Vegas who was accused in August 2024 of plotting a jihad massacre on behalf of the Islamic State (ISIS). After Robles was arrested in November 2023, prosecutors considered him to be so dangerous that they asked that his bail be set at a million dollars; Las Vegas Justice Court Pro Temp Judge Lauren Diefenbach, however, instead decided to set it at $10,000, adding that "should Robles post bail, he would be placed on house arrest with electronic monitoring."[439]

[439] David Charns, "Photos: Las Vegas teenager allegedly 'pledged allegiance to ISIS,' built bombs, threatened school shooting," KLAS, August 29, 2024, https://www.8newsnow.com/investigators/photos-las-vegas-teenager-allegedly-pledged-allegiance-to-isis-built-bombs-threatened-school-shooting/. Accessed October 30, 2024.

Ultimately, however, although Robles was only sixteen, he was deemed to be so dangerous that bail was set at $1 million after all. That was a good decision, because soon after this, authorities found a handwritten note in the young aspiring jihadi's cell which included a drawing of an Islamic State flag and the legend, "Welcome with death."[440] This was after a sheet of notebook paper was found in his bedroom at the time of his arrest showing a faithful recreation of the Islamic State flag, which features in Arabic the Islamic profession of faith, "There is no god but Allah and Muhammad is his prophet." Underneath that, the earnest young convert had written in all caps, "DEATH TO JEWS."[441]

Around that time, Robles was proudly posting online about his enthusiasm for his newfound faith: "Peace by [sic] upon all brothers who see this," he wrote. "I am here to announce that I will be starting lone wolf operations in Las Vegas against the enemies of Allah."[442] When police raided his home, they found "components they said could be used to make an explosive device."[443]

Authorities determined that Robles was "building explosive devices similar to the ones that killed three and injured hundreds in the 2013 Boston Marathon bombing."[444] There was some indication that he planned to carry out an arson jihad attack on New Year's Day, 2024. He was also doing online searches for "information and floorplans for Chaparral High School in the east valley."[445] If he had managed to carry out a jihad attack there, police would still be saying that they didn't know his motives.

---

[440] Ibid.
[441] Ibid.
[442] Ibid.
[443] Ibid.
[444] Ibid.
[445] Ibid.

Prosecutors explained that Robles' "radicalization to violent extremist has developed over several years and continues despite his detention status."[446] It was actually no surprise that Robles continued to demonstrate that he was a jihadi even while in prison. America's prison system, like every other institution in the country, is committed to the proposition that Islam is entirely peaceful and benign. Nothing whatsoever is done to disabuse young men like Robles of their jihadist sentiments; instead, such inmates are given Qur'ans and allowed to pray regularly with other Muslim inmates. Authorities think this will help them discover the true, peaceful Islam. Instead, it all too often breeds more hardened jihadis.

Robles had been a bad actor for quite a while. "In 2020, while in junior high, defendant threatened to shoot up the school. In March of 2023, defendant was created a list of ISIS leader and pledged allegiance to ISIS. He also announced the creation of a local terrorist cell. By May of 2023, Defendant was advising an unknown individual on how to obtain news on ISIS through email and was giving instructions on how to travel in the Middle East."[447] Yet while authorities knew all about all this, none of them seemed to care where or how he converted to Islam, or about how he came to believe that his new religion required him to do violence to non-Muslims.

Until such issues are addressed, and addressed realistically, we will see many more young men like Joshua Robles.

---

446 Ibid.

447 Ibid.

"SALMAN RUSHDIE HAD IT COMING AND 11 OTHER SONGS"?

This is not to say that all converts to Islam become jihadis. Most, obviously, do not. Yet a startlingly large number of converts do, and this stands in contrast to the fact that absolutely no converts to Christianity have become terrorists.

Nevertheless, some converts become, or remain, pillars of the community. The revered former pop star and Muslim convert Cat Stevens (now Yusuf Islam), after years of silence due to his new religion's traditional prohibition of music, returned to public performance and cultivated a gentle persona befitting a man who had once sung a song entitled "Peace Train."

As a zealous new convert, however, he had not always sought to maintain his image as a man of peace. In 2007, *New York Times* interviewer Deborah Solomon asked Yusuf/Cat, "What do you think of Hamas?"[448] It was a simple question, but the former pop crooner appeared flustered, responding, "That's an extremely loaded question."[449] Doggedly, the interviewer asked him, "Can you try to answer it?"[450] Stevens/Islam then said evasively, "I have never supported a terrorist group or any group that did other than charity and good to humankind."[451]

He did not say, of course, that Hamas was a terrorist group, or a group that did anything other than "good to humankind," so Solomon refused to let the question go. "O.K., but many of us here in the States would like to see moderate Muslims make

---

[448] Deborah Solomon, "Questions For Yusuf Islam; Singing a New Song," New York Times, January 7, 2007, https://www.nytimes.com/2007/01/07/magazine/07WWLN_Q4.t.html. Accessed October 31, 2024.

[449] Ibid.

[450] Ibid.

[451] Ibid.

more of an effort to denounce the extremist fringe of the faith. Very few mainstream Muslims have publicly criticized their radical brethren."[452]

Although he had just declined to do exactly that, Yusuf Islam replied, "If I am not an example of that, then tell me, Who is?"[453] Solomon then asked, "So would you say you have contempt for a terrorist group like Hamas?"[454] Again Yusuf declined to condemn this group that celebrated the murders of innocent civilians: "I wouldn't put those words in my mouth. I wouldn't say anything on that issue. I'm here to talk about peace. I'm a man who does want peace for this world, and I don't think you will achieve that by putting people into corners and asking them very, very difficult questions about very contentious issues."[455]

By 2023, the singer was calling himself Yusuf/Cat Stevens, eschewing the monicker he had used since his conversion. An Associated Press report happily announced that "the 'Peace Train' hitmaker worked for years on the 12 new songs, revisiting familiar themes," including ones of "togetherness."[456] AP also notes that "the first single is the cheerful, family friendly 'Take the World Apart,' with the lyrics 'I'll take the world apart/to find a place for a peaceful heart.'"[457]

All this sounded a great deal like the old hippie Cat Stevens from the late 1960s and early 1970s, but oddities and questions lingered. The *Washington Post* reminded the world that in 2021,

---

452 Ibid.

453 Ibid.

454 Ibid.

455 Ibid.

456 Mark Kennedy, "Cat Stevens to return this summer with a new album," Associated Press, https://www.newscentermaine.com/article/news/nation-world/cat-stevens-new-album-king-of-a-land/507-22bf25ca-9853-490d-a1f8-f6852f92f70a. Accessed October 31, 2024.

457 Ibid.

when Cat Stevens was first reemerging after decades of silence, as a new convert to Islam he enthusiastically endorsed the death fatwa against Salman Rushdie for supposedly blaspheming Muhammad, the prophet of Islam. In 1989, "after Rushdie had officially been targeted because of his portrayal of the prophet Muhammad in his novel 'The Satanic Verses,' Stevens had matter-of-factly confirmed that the Koran prescribes death as the punishment for blasphemy."[458]

Nor was this simply a matter of confirming that the death penalty for blasphemy was indeed Islamic teaching. Confronted on a BBC show, "Stevens was asked directly whether Rushdie deserved to die. 'Yes, yes,' he replied, without much hesitation. Were Rushdie, a marked man, to come to him for help, how would he respond? With what he subsequently insisted was nothing more than an ill-advised attempt at dry humor, a straight-faced Stevens said: 'I might ring somebody who might do more damage to him than he would like. I'd try to phone the Ayatollah Khomeini and tell him exactly where this man is.' When asked whether he would participate in the burning of an effigy of the author, he replied that he would instead hope it were 'the real thing.'"[459]

When the predictable firestorm ensued, Cat Stevens/Yusuf Islam issued a press release "indicating that his comments had been manipulated in the editing room and taken out of context" (despite the fact that the *New York Times* reported that Stevens had "watched a preview of the program today and said in an

---

458 Howard Fishman, "The Meaning of Yusuf/Cat Stevens," Washington Post, September 20, 2021, https://www.washingtonpost.com/magazine/2021/09/20/yusufcat-stevens-reemerges-public-stage-how-should-we-feel-about-his-music-his-legacy/?itid=hp_dont-miss. Accessed October 31, 2024.

459 Ibid.

interview that he stood by his comments"[460]). On his official website, he makes a patently false claim: "I never called for the death of Salman Rushdie; nor backed the Fatwa issued by the Ayatollah Khomeini—and still don't."[461] In the very next sentence, he blames Rushdie's book, not Khomeini's fatwa, for all the trouble: "The book itself destroyed the harmony between people and nations and created an international crisis."[462]

Salman Rushdie himself would have none of Stevens' denials, saying, "For many years, Yusuf Islam has been pretending he didn't say the things he said in 1989, when he enthusiastically supported the Iranian terrorist edict against me and others. However, his words are on the record, in print interviews and on television programs.... I'm afraid Cat Stevens got off the peace train a long time ago."[463]

Indeed. As recently as 2010, there was published on YouTube a *nasheed*—an a cappella Islamic hymn that is often a call to jihad (which in some Muslim schools of thought is the only kind of music that is allowed)—in which the author of "Peace Train" sang, "I'm praying to Allah to give us victory over the kuffar" (unbelievers).[464] Does Yusuf/Cat still pray for victory over the kuffar? What kind of victory?

In 2004, Yusuf Islam was barred from entering the United States because of suspicions that he had been financing jihad terrorism (the ban was later lifted). He acknowledged that some of his money may have gone to jihadis, but he claimed to have

---

460 Ibid.

461 "Editing Floor Blues," Yusuf/Cat Stevens, https://catstevens.com/editing-floor-blues/. Accessed October 31, 2024.

462 Ibid.

463 Fishman, "The Meaning of Yusuf/Cat Stevens," op. cit.

464 Yusuf Islam, "Turn to Allah (Where Are You Going)," YouTube video, December 11, 2010, https://www.youtube.com/watch?v=belycDxH9KE. Accessed October 31, 2024.

given money to them unwittingly: "It's possible that sometimes during the distribution process help may have reached people or their families who were deemed as politically or religiously unsavoury by certain regimes, but that does not necessarily prove a case for supporting terrorism or violence."[465] Of course.

But today no one cares about all that. Fans eagerly snapped up Yusuf/Cat's new album and rode the peace train once again, just like in the days when they claimed to constitute a "free speech movement." But the lingering question remains: didn't their hero, whom they thought was driving that peace train, get off that train many years ago?

465 "Editing Floor Blues," op. cit.

CHAPTER NINETEEN

SHAME AND HONOR

COGNITIVE DISSONANCE

Ultimately, all the fictional converts to Islam and fantasies about great Islamic achievements of the past ring hollow: the failure of Islamic societies is still a manifest fact. Those who live in those societies can't help but be reminded of it every day. Meanwhile, Islam inculcates contempt for those who shower billions upon the Islamic world in order to improve it economically, socially, and culturally, for they are the most vile of created beings who will never be satisfied with the Muslims, the best of peoples, until they forsake Islam and convert to Judaism or Christianity.

Yet the fact that the vile infidels continue to outstrip the best of peoples in intellectual achievements and societal advances remains a tremendous source of shame. Shame leads to hatred for the source of the shame, and the imperative to strike back. Raphael Patai notes "the drive to restore damaged honor, to 'whiten the face' that has been 'blackened' by having been dishonored and shamed."[466] In Islamic cultures, he states, "any injury done to a man's honor must be revenged, or else he becomes permanently dishonored."[467]

In this context, Patai continues,

> there is no greater shame than defeat by an enemy, and especially an enemy such as Israel, the Jews, who ever since the days of Muhammad have been looked down upon by the Arabs as *dhimmis*, a people brought low and subjected as well as protected by Islam. If it is Allah's will that the Arabs be defeated by such an enemy, or any enemy, it is up to them to plan patiently for the revenge which alone can restore their honor, even if they have to wait for it for years or, if need be, decades. When the attainment of such a supreme value is the goal, the pressure to achieve it mounts until it is strong enough to overcome the threat-inaction pattern. Examples of such occurrences abound in past Arab history.[468]

This shame must be avenged because it can neither be explained nor escaped. The Qur'an promises that those who obey Allah will be rewarded in this world as well as the next. Unaware of the idea of the wicked prospering, it frees the faithful from having to grapple with the theological implications of evil people appearing to enjoy the blessings of the Almighty. That theological simplicity, however, renders the Muslims' defeat, especially at the hands of Jews—whom the Qur'an says are "the

466 Patai, The Arab Mind, op. cit., xxiii.
467 Ibid.
468 Ibid.

most vehement of mankind in hostility to those who believe" (5:82)—absolutely inexplicable.

This is why revenge is the only option. The shame must be avenged. On October 7, 2023, as it began its massacre of 1,200 Israelis, Hamas issued a statement proclaiming that "the moment of revenge for our martyrs has come, and those who wronged will know which side to turn against."[469] Revenge for what? Answers have been various: the alleged theft of land, the supposed occupation, the claimed atrocities that Israel has been charged with committing against Palestinians. Ultimately, however, the imperative for revenge will remain as long as Israel exists, no matter how many concessions it ultimately makes to the hostile jihadi entities that surround and menace it.

ISRAEL'S EXISTENCE IS AN INSULT TO ISLAM

The very existence of Israel is a source of tremendous shame in the Islamic world. It contradicts Islam's theology in not granting victory to the pious Muslims. Even worse, it is a functioning and reasonably prosperous society in a sea of less functional Muslim Arab states, yet is run by those whom the Qur'an says were transformed into apes and pigs for their disobedience to Allah (2:63–6; 5:59–60; 7:166).

Over the years, Israel has made innumerable overtures to the neighboring Arab and Muslim states on the basis of their common interests. In 2018, longtime Israeli Prime Minister Benjamin Netanyahu even reached out to the Iranian people, offering them

[469] "Hamas, Islamic Jihad, Lions' Den Threaten Lone Wolf Attacks, Claim Capture Of Israeli Soldiers, Call On Palestinians To Disable Surveillance Systems As Part Of Ongoing Operation Against Israel," MEMRI, October 7, 2023, https://www.memri.org/reports/hamas-islamic-jihad-lions-den-threaten-lone-wolf-attacks-claim-capture-israeli-soldiers-call. Accessed October 30, 2024.

Israeli expertise in water management in a time of drought. "The Iranian people," Netanyahu observed, "are the victims of a cruel and tyrannical regime that denies them vital water. Israel stands with the people of Iran, and that is why I want to save countless Iranian lives."[470] He explained, "Israel has the know-how to prevent environmental catastrophe in Iran. I want to share this information with the people of Iran."[471]

If the Iranian leadership had seen fit to accept the offer, Iran could have been transformed for the better. Netanyahu noted that "Iran's meteorological organization says that nearly 96 percent of Iran suffers from some levels of drought. Issa Kalantari, a former Iranian agriculture minister, said that 50 million Iranians could be forced out of their homes due to environmental damage. 50 million!"[472]

Yet there was never any chance that Iran would respond favorably to this offer, no matter how beneficial accepting it might have been for the Iranian people. Getting help from the "Little Satan" Israel, upon whom the Iranian leadership regularly wished death, was absolutely out of the question. It was better for the Iranian people to suffer than to accept aid from Israel. This was a longstanding policy of the Islamic Republic. In 1990, after an earthquake devastated Iran, the Iranian government welcomed humanitarian aid from any and all nations, with two notable exceptions: Israel and apartheid South Africa.

Not only was the Islamic Republic of Iran deeply and unshakably hostile to the Jewish state, but even if there had been friendly or simply neutral relations between the two countries, to accept

---

470 "Netanyahu offers Israeli water tech to Iran," Times of Israel, June 10, 2018, https://www.timesofisrael.com/netanyahu-offers-israeli-water-tech-to-solve-irans-growing-environmental-crisis/. Accessed October 30, 2024.

471 Ibid.

472 Ibid.

Israeli help would have been an intolerable new source of dishonor. These were the people whom the Qur'an said were the most hostile to the Muslims. These were those who would never be satisfied with the Muslims unless and until they discarded their Islam and embraced Judaism.

Iran was not alone in this stance. The *Jerusalem Post* reported in February 2022 that "since the devastating explosion of Beirut's port in the summer of 2020 and the ongoing financial crisis, Jerusalem has offered aid to Beirut multiple times including to the Lebanese Armed Forces."[473] However, "Israel never received any response from international agencies and organizations after the country issued numerous offers of aid to Lebanon."[474]

When a massive earthquake struck Turkey and Syria in February 2023, Israel offered aid to both countries. Turkey accepted it, although its president, Recep Tayyip Erdogan, tempered the shame of this acceptance by continuing his hostile rhetoric against the Jewish state, and his party's newspaper, *Yeni Safak*, declared about Israel that "the terror state must be destroyed."[475] Syrian President Bashar al-Assad, meanwhile, rejected Israel's offer of aid, while quietly allowing Israeli humanitarian teams to go to work inside the country.[476] The public rejection of the Israeli aid, while some of this aid was actually accepted, was apparently

---

473 Anna Ahronheim, "Lebanon never refused Israeli aid, they just never responded," Jerusalem Post, February 17, 2022, https://www.jpost.com/middle-east/article-696796. Accessed October 30, 2024.

474 Ibid.

475 Hugh Fitzgerald, "Israel Should Stop Sending Aid to its Enemies," Jihad Watch, February 7, 2024, https://jihadwatch.org/2024/02/israel-should-stop-sending-aid-to-its-enemies. Accessed October 30, 2024.

476 Nir Boms and Joelle Rosenthal, "Regional Crisis and Regional Cooperation: Israeli Response to the Earthquake in Syria and Turkey," Fikra Forum, Washington Institute for Near East Policy, March 6, 2023, https://www.washingtoninstitute.org/policy-analysis/regional-crisis-and-regional-cooperation-israeli-response-earthquake-syria-and. Accessed October 27, 2024.

sufficient to allow al-Assad to evade the shame of receiving help from the hated Jews.

A THEOLOGICAL IMPERATIVE

The theological underpinnings that the Qur'an and Islamic tradition provide for hatred and fear of the Jews means that this contempt for Israel and refusal to cooperate with it, even for their own benefit, can never end. It can't be negotiated away with a signed agreement. It can't be tempered or moderated or modernized or nuanced. The Qur'an is the perfect word of Allah that has existed with him in paradise for all eternity. How could the reasoning of mere mortals supersede the word of the one and only god?

The hatred of Israel stems not from Israeli policies, but from what Israel is in its essence. The hatred of the United States, in exactly the same way, stems also from its status as an infidel polity, but in Israel's case the hatred is even more intense, because Israel is the Jewish state. Post-Christian Westerners generally have a hard time understanding the religious imperative. They assume that everyone across the globe is animated by the same humanistic assumptions that drive them, and so they assume that Muslims will be glad to come to some accord with infidels that will ensure peaceful coexistence.

This is not and has never been the case. As Muhammad said, "Islam must dominate and is not to be dominated."[477] Muslims may make agreements with infidel states on the basis of a shared short-term goal or to face a common enemy, but these can never and will never override Islamic imperatives. The success of the

---

477 Sahih Al-Jami 2778

West, along with the success of Israel, are sources of tremendous shame for the Islamic world, but the answer for all too many Muslims is not to study the secrets of the West's success and try to emulate them, but to ratchet up hostility toward those whose day-to-day lives contradict the eternal assertions of Islam, and ultimately to destroy them. That destruction will prove once again that Allah is indeed *akbar*, the greater.

THE PERFECTION OF ISLAM

If the West is successful and the Islamic world is not, both Westerners and Muslims will agree that the problem is not Islam.

Westerners, forever indulging in their endless orgy of self-recriminations and self-reproach, wouldn't dream of being so "racist" as to suggest that the problem with the Islamic world might be Islam itself, and that it contains teachings that inculcate assumptions and attitudes that retard human progress. They work to boost Muslim self-esteem by imagining a mythical past in which Islam was both great and magnanimous, and when its thinkers, inventors and explorers were unmatched anywhere in the world.

Pious Muslims, meanwhile, are certain that Islam is perfect, because Islam tells them that it is. "This day I have perfected your religion for you," says Allah to the believers in the Qur'an, and completed my favor to you, and have chosen Islam as the religion for you. Whoever is forced by hunger to sin against his will, indeed, Allah is forgiving, merciful." (5:3) If Islam is perfect, it doesn't need to be changed, reformed, or adapted to modern conditions. It certainly doesn't need to be subjected to Western non-Muslim critique. The very idea of such things would be an insult to Allah, who assures Muslims that their religion has no flaws and thus cannot be improved.

Why, then, are the believers not prospering as Allah promised? Why are the hated infidels, the most vile of created beings, surpassing the faithful in so many ways? These are questions that, like others, must not be asked, for the answers might shake one's faith. The Qur'an specifically rules out such inquiries: "O you who believe, do not ask about things which, if they were made known to you, would trouble you.… A people before you asked, and then became unbelievers." (5:101–2).

This was the diametric opposite of the New Testament's exhortation to the believers to be ready to defend their faith, which would necessarily involve dealing with difficult questions: "Always be prepared to make a defense to anyone who calls you to account for the hope that is in you, yet do it with gentleness and reverence." (I Peter 3:15).

The gulf between those mindsets was as large as the gulf between the civilizations built upon these two faiths.

CHAPTER TWENTY

SOLD OUT

THE TIKTOK CONVERSION CRAZE

It would be one of the supreme ironies of history if the West embraced Islam just as Iran and other areas of the Islamic world were liberating themselves from it. But it could easily happen. After the Hamas jihad massacre of 1,200 Israelis on October 7, 2023, social media "influencers" on the popular app TikTok discovered Osama bin Laden's 2002 letter to the American people, in which he called on Americans to embrace Islam. National Public Radio reported in November 2023 that "hundreds of videos" had appeared featuring people reading the letter in whole or part, and praising Osama.[478] One stated, "Everyone should read it.... However, be forewarned that this has left me very disillusioned."[479] Another said, "I will never look

[478] Bobby Allyn, "The story behind the Osama bin Laden videos on TikTok," National Public Radio, November 17, 2023, https://www.npr.org/2023/11/17/1213712136/tik-tok-bin-laden-videos-osama. Accessed October 30, 2024.

[479] Ibid.

at life the same. I will never look at this country the same. Please read it."[480]

After the Osama craze, came a spate of TikTok videos featuring "influencers" announcing and celebrating their conversions to Islam. This fad was to some degree the result of well over twenty years of relentless indoctrination from the educational system and the media. In the wake of the jihad attacks on September 11, 2001, children in America were not taught about Islamic jihad and its global threat to the free world, but about the dangers of "Islamophobia." Public school textbooks taught a generation of children about the evils perpetrated by Jews and Christians, but carefully presented Islam in a uniformly positive light, so as not to incite "anti-Muslim bigotry."

A generation of schoolchildren, therefore, grew up with the idea that the foundational religions of the Western world were tainted and corrupt, and were used as instruments of oppression. Judaism was in the background of the alleged oppressiveness of the state of Israel, and the history of Europe was presented as one long act of "liberation" from Christianity. When what they had taught seemed to come to life in the aftermath of the October 7 attacks, it was no surprise that they would look to Islam as a panacea. No one among these young enthusiasts, of course, asked any young people in Iran what they thought of this idea.

Because of the relentless public relations campaign that has been carried out all over the West ever since 9/11, supposedly to guard against "Islamophobia," few Americans or Europeans of any age are aware of why the Iranians would be so disenchanted with Islam after forty years of Islamic rule. Even fewer have any idea of why Islamic societies are uniformly failures. Whenever

[480] Ibid.

anyone gets close to the truth of these matters, a leftist or Muslim spokesman has an excuse ready: the failure of Islam is because of Israel, or colonialism, or racism, or a biased media, or any number of other excuses that are crafted to appeal to ill-informed and miseducated young leftists of the early twenty-first century.

Sometimes those excuses are quite elaborate and sophisticated. But for all that, they are still just excuses, attempts to cover for what by now is obvious to anyone who is willing to see it: Islam is a failure. It has failed everywhere it has been tried, and has failed comprehensively.

Yet it looks as if Europe has decided to give it another try.

AN ISLAMIC EUROPE

Several years ago, while in Israel, I took a tour of the ancient city of Caesarea. Part of the tour consisted of maps projected onto the wall of the city as it appeared under the rule of the Roman Empire; the Roman empire in Constantinople, also known as the Byzantine Empire; the Arabs; the Crusaders; the Ottoman Turks; and the Israelis. The city was thriving in four of these epochs, but became a backwater and a ghost town in two: under the Arabs and the Turks, the only periods during which the city was under the rule of Islamic law. The tour leaders did not remark on this fact, much less attempt to explain it, but it was obvious from the maps they displayed.

Was this just coincidence, or did Islam somehow cause the city's decline?

It may be too late for anyone in the Western world to be asking such questions. As early as 2004, the renowned historian Bernard Lewis made a startling prediction, evincing no uncertainty about it whatsoever. "Europe," Lewis declared, "will be Islamic by the end of the century."[481]

Lewis was so sure of this because the groundwork for Europe's Islamization had begun to be laid decades before. As far back as 1973, the European Union began to construct what the historian Bat Ye'or called "a whole infrastructure of alliances and economic, industrial, media, cultural, financial bonds with the countries of the Arab League."[482] This new Euro-Muslim entity—which its architects called "Eurabia"—was meant to become "a counterweight to American power" worldwide, and also would attempt "to separate and weaken the two continents by an incitement to hostility and the permanent denigration of American policy in the Middle East."[483]

Bat Ye'or noted that this initiative grew out of the oil crisis of the early 1970s:

> After the Yom Kippur War and the Arab oil blackmail in 1973, the then-European Community (EC) created a structure of Cooperation and Dialogue with the Arab League. The Euro-Arab Dialogue (EAD) began as a French initiative composed of representatives from the EC and Arab League countries. From the outset the EAD was considered as a vast transaction: The EC agreed to support the Arab anti-Israeli policy in exchange for wide commercial agreements.

481 "Europa wird am Ende des Jahrhunderts islamisch sein," Die Welt, July 28, 2004, http://www.trafoberlin.de/pdf-dateien/Bernard%20Lewis%20Islamisches%20Europa%20Juli%202004.pdf. Accessed October 30, 2024.

482 Robert Spencer, "The Rise of 'Eurabia," FrontPage Magazine, March 30, 2004, https://swap.stanford.edu/was/20090618203455/http://www.frontpagemagazine.com/readArticle.aspx?ARTID=13756. Accessed October 29, 2024.

483 Ibid.

> The EAD had a supplementary function: the shifting of Europe into the Arab-Islamic sphere of influence, thus breaking the traditional trans-Atlantic solidarity. The EAD operated at the highest political level, with foreign ministers on both sides, and the presidents of the EC—later the European Union (EU)—with the secretary general of the Arab League. The central body of the Dialogue, the General Commission, was responsible for planning its objectives in the political, cultural, social, economic, and technological domains; it met in private, without summary records, a common practice for European meetings.[484]

In 1983, Foreign Minister Hans-Dietrich Genscher of West Germany explained what his government hoped would result from this dialogue:

> The Euro-Arab Dialogue would indeed remain incomplete if the political side were to be ignored or not taken seriously. Both parties to the Dialogue, both partners, should always remind themselves of the joint Memorandum issued in Cairo in 1975, the Charter of the Dialogue. The Memorandum contains the following quote: "The Euro-Arab Dialogue is the outcome of the common political will which strives for the creation of a special relationship between the

[484] Bat Ye'or, "Eurabia: The Road to Munich," in The Myth of Islamic Tolerance: How Islamic Law Treats Non-Muslims, ed. Robert Spencer (Amherst, New York: Prometheus Books, 2004), 290.

> two groups." We Europeans spoke out in a clear and convinced manner for a revival of the Euro-Arab Dialogue in the Vienna Declaration of June 13, 1980. Since then, the various working groups within the Dialogue have become more active and the prospects for the future are more promising.
>
> Our Arab partners in the Dialogue have also indicated that they are in favour of continuing and intensifying this Dialogue. Both in the course of this joint venture, our Symposium, and through its outcome, it will become clear that we are determined to give the Euro-Arab Dialogue a new and long-lease of life.[485]

That was exactly what happened, as Bat Ye'or explains, "Europe's economic greed was instrumentalized by Arab League policy in a long-term political strategy targeting Israel, Europe, and America."[486]

Fifty years after it began, the idea of Eurabia is deeply embedded in the policies of the European Union. Bat Ye'or points out that "over the years, Euro-Arab collaboration developed at all levels: political, economic, religious and in the transfer of technologies, education, universities, radio, television, press, publishers, and writers unions. This structure became the channel for Arab immigration into Europe, of anti-Americanism, and of Judeophobia, which—linked with a general hatred of the West and its denigration—constituted a pseudo-culture imported

[485] Ibid., 290–291.
[486] Ibid., 291.

from Arab countries. The interpenetration of European and Arab policies determined Europe's relentless anti-Israel policy and its anti-Americanism. This politico-economic edifice, with minute details, is rooted in a multiform European symbiosis with the Arab world."[487]

Europe received oil and access to markets in the Arab world. In return, they agreed to mass Arab and Muslim migration into Europe, without assimilation. All this happened, however, behind the backs of most of the population of Europe. According to Bat Ye'or, "beyond a fleeting awareness, the overwhelming majority of Europeans and Americans do not understand the new Eurabian entity, which is only the first step in a steady progression toward its Arabization and Islamization. Europe has evolved from a Judeo-Christian civilization, with important post-Enlightenment/secular elements, to a 'civilization of dhimmitude,' i.e., Eurabia: a secular-Muslim transitional society with its traditional Judeo-Christian mores rapidly disappearing."[488]

This is not an accident; it is part of the plan. Bat Ye'or added that "this program of Euro-Arab symbiosis has been codified in a detailed report entitled, 'Dialogue between Peoples and Cultures in the Euro-Mediterranean Area.'" Released in October 2003, "this report (whose contributors included [renowned novelist] Umberto Eco and [influential Islamic intellectual and later convicted rapist] Tariq Ramadan) was to establish complete interdependence between Europe and the Arab-Muslim world."[489] "Complete," as in, encompassing every aspect of life.

---

[487] Ibid., 290.

[488] Ibid.

[489] Bat Ye'or, "How Europe Became Eurabia," Jihad Watch, July 27, 2004, https://jihadwatch.org/2004/07/how-europe-became-eurabia. Accessed October 29, 2024.

"One can choose to ignore it," Bat Ye'or stated, "but Eurabia is a tangible entity. Eurabia has a discernible historical development, and its functionaries are now well entrenched in each European parliament, and at the head of the European Commission."[490]

THE DEATH OF EUROPE

Bat Ye'or explained that destroying Europe's culture as it had been constituted for centuries was all part of the plan:

> A wide-ranging policy was then first sketched out, a symbiosis of Europe with the Muslim Arab countries, that would endow Europe—and especially France, the project's prime mover—with a weight and a prestige to rival that of the United States. This policy was undertaken quite discreetly, outside of official treaties, under the innocent-sounding name of the Euro-Arab Dialogue. An association of European parliamentarians from the European Economic Community (EEC) was created in 1974 in Paris: the Parliamentary Association for Euro-Arab Cooperation. It was entrusted with managing all of the aspects of Euro-Arab relations—financial, political, economic, cultural, and those pertaining to immigration. This organization functioned under the auspices of the European heads of government and their foreign ministers, working in close association with their Arab counterparts, and with the

[490] Ibid.

representatives of the European Commission, and the Arab League.

This strategy, the goal of which was the creation of a pan-Mediterranean Euro-Arab entity, permitting the free circulation both of men and of goods, also determined the immigration policy with regard to Arabs in the European Community (EC). And, for the past 30 years, it also established the relevant cultural policies in the schools and universities of the EC. Since the first Cairo meeting of the Euro-Arab Dialogue in 1975, attended by the ministers and heads of state both from European and Arab countries and by representatives of the EC and the Arab League, agreements have been concluded concerning the diffusion and the promotion in Europe of Islam, of the Arabic language and culture, through the creation of Arab cultural centers in European cities. Other accords soon followed, all intended to ensure a cultural, economic, political Euro-Arab symbiosis. These far ranging efforts involved the universities and the media (both written and audio-visual), and even included the transfer of technologies, including nuclear technology. Finally a Euro-Arab associative diplomacy was promoted in international forums, especially at the United Nations.[491]

[491] Bat Ye'or, "Beyond Munich: The Spirit of Eurabia," in The Myth of Islamic Tolerance, op. cit., 284–285.

In line with this vision, French President Nicolas Sarkozy in 2007 advocated a "Union for the Mediterranean," which would, he said happily, "change the world."[492] Sarkozy envisioned an accord between the countries of Europe and North Africa that would give Muslims from Algeria, Morocco and Libya significant power and influence in Europe.

In Germany, Chancellor Angela Merkel was determined not to fail. The transformation of Europe was already well under way when German Chancellor Angela Merkel gave it a significant boost on August 31, 2015. Announcing that she was opening Germany's doors to mass migration, she enunciated a warning, "If Europe fails on the question of refugees, if this close link with universal civil rights is broken, then it won't be the Europe we wished for."[493] Eight hundred thousand migrants took advantage of Merkel's hospitality in 2015; millions more have entered the country since then. This must have pleased Merkel, for she explained that it gave Germany a new reputation before the world: "The world sees Germany as a country of hope and opportunity, that was not always the case." Opponents of the mass migration enterprise would be crushed: "There is no tolerance for those who question the dignity of other people." Calling on the Germans to support her migration initiative, she uttered the now-famous slogan: "We can do it!"[494]

---

492 Navtej Dhillon, The 'Union for the Mediterranean:' The Next Generation of Europe-Middle East Cooperation?," Brookings, August 14, 2008, https://www.brookings.edu/articles/the-union-for-the-mediterranean-the-next-generation-of-europe-middle-east-cooperation/. Accessed October 30, 2024.

493 Melissa Eddy, "Angela Merkel Calls for European Unity to Address Migrant Influx," New York Times, August 31, 2015, https://www.nytimes.com/2015/09/01/world/europe/germany-migrants-merkel.html. Accessed October 30, 2024.

494 Justin Huggler, "Merkel defiant over refugee policy: 'we can do it,'" Telegraph, August 31, 2016, https://www.telegraph.co.uk/news/2016/08/31/merkel-defiant-over-refugee-policy-we-can-do-it/. Accessed October 30, 2024.

But could Germany really do it? And should Germany really have done it?

In January 2020, a German opposition MP, Gottfried Curio of the Alternative for Germany (AfD) party, confronted Merkel: "Madame Chancellor, on the recent violence in Augsburg, where a group of young migrants killed one man and seriously injured another—this wasn't a terror attack, but a spontaneous outbreak of violence, which doesn't make it better. Actually, it's worse, because it makes it more commonplace. The perpetrators of Augsburg were born there and in the second generation are living according to the typical norms of internalized machismo. They see it as honorable and strong to exercise violence. Such people turn the public space into a place of fear, a place where the fist rules. So much for the integration fairy tale. The Federal Report on Immigrant Crime shows that Augsburg is the tip of the iceberg. The immigrant perpetrators have multiplied dramatically since 2014. Last year, hundreds of cases of murder and manslaughter, thousands of cases of sexual assault, tens of thousands of cases of bodily injury. In light of such numbers, of migrant criminals, would you speak of isolated incidents, or do you recognize that there are systemic problems?"[495]

Merkel, a seasoned politician, knew better than to answer the question on its own terms. "First of all," she replied, "I recognize that a terrible crime was committed in Augsburg and that naturally our thoughts are with the relatives and also with those who were injured. Secondly, I recognize that the government is called upon to combat all forms of violence wherever they occur. We are also working to constantly improve our opportunities for

495 "German Parliament Erupts as Merkel vows to combat migrant crimes by fighting 'Right-Wing Extremists,'" RAIR Foundation USA, January 21, 2020, https://altcensored.com/watch?v=UPML1sin6hQ. Accessed October 30, 2024.

action, for example by creating a large number of new positions in the fight against right-wing extremism. Of course, we are also working in other areas, and we will of course continue this work, but overall I believe our constitutional state is capable of acting at both the federal and state levels."[496]

When Merkel spoke about "right-wing extremism," many of the elected representatives who were in the chamber could not contain their laughter. This was because the attackers in Augsburg were not "right-wing extremists" at all, but Muslims whose parents had come to Germany. Merkel spoke of "right-wing extremism" because that was a problem she recognized and was only too happy to confront; Islamic jihad, however, and the contempt that all too many Muslims, as "the best of people" (Qur'an 3:110) had for the laws and customs of the "most vile of created beings" (Qur'an 98:6), were not issues that Merkel or anyone else in the Western intelligentsia was prepared to recognize.

Curio no doubt knew this, but nonetheless, he continued to press Merkel. "From 2014 to 2018," he stated, "there were over 800,000 immigrant crimes, and these are just the solved ones. Including the estimated unreported cases, there are millions of crimes that could have been prevented by border security. Do you recognize that you are personally at fault for the continued intake of this high-risk group of young male migrants having an Islamic and clan culture? It was and still is completely unnecessary, because this occurs via self-admittance permitted on the basis of an alleged emergency situation, which is now being used

---

[496] Ibid.

for a permanent resettlement. Do you recognize your personal responsibility?"[497]

Merkel responded with characteristic evasiveness, "The Federal Chancellor is always responsible for the political events in the country. I'm also glad that I am allowed to hold such an important office. Secondly, there are different views regarding what happened in 2015 and in the following years. I believe that Germany has helped a great many people in need, that society as a whole has made an effort to do so, and that we have also, of course, worked and will continue to work on the order and management of migration, and the figures show that this work is not in vain, but that it has been successful."[498]

The German government was anxious to continue its mass migration program. In April 2020, even when much of Europe was in lockdown over the COVID-19 hysteria, Germany's Minister of Justice and Anti-Discrimination in Berlin, Dirk Behrendt, argued that Germany should take in even more migrants: "We have a lot of vacant hotels in Berlin that could also be used to accommodate refugees. We have capacities."[499] Referring to an overcrowded refugee camp in Greece, Behrendt continued: "The fact that the people of Lesbos live in makeshift tents in the rain and cold is unworthy of the European Union."[500]

What was worthy of the European Union, evidently, was its demographic conquest and Islamization. Whether or not this will prove to be a civilizational advance remains to be seen. It is

---

497 Ibid.

498 Ibid.

499 "German Officials Now Pushing to Import Migrants, House Them In Hotels Amid Pandemic," *Demokracija*, April 3, 2020, https://demokracija.eu/migration/https-europe-infowars-com-german-politicians-pushing-to-import-migrants-house-them-in-hotels-amid-pandemic/. Accessed October 30, 2024.

500 Ibid.

unlikely, however, that an Islamic Europe will prove to be significantly different from an Islamic Middle East, an Islamic North Africa, and an Islamic Asia. In fact, insofar as Europe imbibes the Islamic value of relying on others to do the work that is beneath Muslims to do, it will likely cease to be an economic powerhouse, as well as a cultural center.

The effect of Islam will once again be seen on a massive scale, while the remaining non-Muslims cast about for anything to which they can ascribe their decline other than the actual cause of it.

ACKNOWLEDGMENTS

To say that this small book sums up what I've learned in decades of studying Islam and observing its adherents might constitute what kids today, or kids of five minutes ago, would call a "self-own." Nevertheless, it is true that I've tried to express here something that doesn't appear in my other books, and is in large part the fruit of innumerable enlightening discussions that I've had over a lifetime with people who are far more knowledgeable than I.

To list them all would be impossible, but to list a few of them is not intended to insult those who are not mentioned, particularly since there are not a few people around this giddy globe who are genuinely, and not without justification, afraid that public association with me could get them killed, or if not that, then ruined professionally. That's the way the world is today for those who tell the truth, and for alerting me to elements of that truth, I remain everlastingly grateful to the late, great David G. Littman and Oriana Fallaci, as well as to my likewise departed friend Jeffrey Rubin, and to Bat Ye'or, Ibn Warraq, Hugh Fitzgerald, and so many others. Daniel Pipes kindly alerted me to some valuable sources of which I have made extensive use here. Each one of them was or is, as has been said of other people in other contexts, *il miglior fabbro*, but I've done what I could do.

David S. Bernstein of Bombardier Books once again deserves a nod, and more than a nod, for his continuing interest in my books. This is my twelfth Bombardier Book, and I thank David, as well as the ace production managers Aleigha Koss and Lauren Campbell, for remaining patient with me over all these years now. In a darkening world, those who are willing to produce dissident literature, as well as those who dare to read it, are dwindling in number. David and his team deserve the gratitude of all of us for keeping his samizdat press going this long against all odds.